TEACHING MUSIC
WITH PASSION

Conducting, Rehearsing and Inspiring

PETER LOEL BOONSHAFT

Published by
MEREDITH MUSIC PUBLICATIONS
a division of G.W. Music, Inc.
4899 Lerch Creek Ct., Galesville, MD 20765
http://www.meredithmusic.com

MEREDITH MUSIC PUBLICATIONS and its stylized double M logo are trademarks of
MEREDITH MUSIC PUBLICATIONS, a division of G.W. Music, Inc.

Library of Congress Control Number: 2002110678

International Standard Book Number: 0-634-05331-0
Printed and bound in U.S.A

DEDICATION

For my wife Martha, and my children Meredith Ann, Peter Loel and Matthew Christopher. All the best things in my life are you. You are the strength of my being, the source of all my joy, my inspiration for everything, and my window to all that is wondrous and beautiful in the world. You have been, are, and will always be, my greatest passion.

ACKNOWLEDGEMENTS

Dr. Garwood Whaley, for your patience, talents and kindness.

Bruce Bush, for your friendship, support and confidence.

Reber Clark and Nancy Bittner, for your wisdom, sincerity and counsel.

Dr. Tim Lautzenheiser, for your encouragement, spirit and enthusiasm. Words do not exist that are powerful enough to express my appreciation to you, my friend, for writing the foreword for this book. Thank you.

My family, friends and colleagues, for your thoughtfulness, insight and inspiration.

And most importantly, all of my students, who have given me the privilege and honor of learning from them. The happiness you have brought me is only surpassed by my gratitude for all of you.

Contents

FOREWORD

From the pen of Dr. Peter Loel Boonshaft blooms a wonderful gift, *Teaching Music with Passion*. The book's title understates the powerful message Peter brings to our teaching forum; his knowledgeable perspective highlights every aspect of the teacher/conductor's responsibility.

The following pages offer a wealth of information cleverly blended with Dr. Boonshaft's personal experiences during his successful tenure as a music educator, college professor, and (above all) an extremely gifted conductor. He is one of those exemplary role models who "walks his talk." The book represents a lifetime-of-learning he unselfishly documents and contributes to our professional library.

In his own words, "Keep it all in perspective; the moment, the rehearsal, and the year. Remember what's really important; that they love and appreciate music, themselves and their world. With your guidance, patience and example, they will." To this end Peter takes the reader on an awareness journey; he embraces a critical viewpoint of our demand for excellence both on and off the podium while linking the importance of developing every aspect of life to fulfill our teaching mission.

I applaud Dr. Boonshaft for sharing his own anecdotal experiences. Not only do they bring a sense of realness to his message, but they afford us the opportunity to see what powerful stepping stones these instances offer to every teacher's evolution. You will be amused (as only a musician can be) and delighted with the many personal tales, and you will find yourself nodding-in-agreement as you relate to similar situations in your own career.

Teaching Music with Passion is a book you will want to read from cover-to-cover, in that it has a capturing quality that entices the reader to keep turning the pages. However, you will be best served to consume the text in small bites, chewing each thought and savoring every morsel of thought-provocation. I dare say you will find yourself re-reading various pages for there is as much written "between the lines" as "on the lines."

Above all, Peter gently avails us to the importance of *the messenger* as well as *the message*. As written in the postlude, quoting Shari Lewis, "As teachers, you will teach as much with who you are as with what you know," he pinpoints the key to becoming a master teacher.

A hearty BRAVO is extended to Dr. Peter Loel Boonshaft; we are the benefactors of his tried-and-true understanding and his heartfelt wisdom.

THANK YOU, MY FRIEND.

Let the music begin....

—Tim Lautzenheiser

PREFACE:
A CORNER, A CONGRESSMAN
AND AN OYSTER

You may be asking yourself what these three things could possibly have in common. And even if they do have something in common, what could they have to do with the teaching of music? Simply, each word represents a quote. Allow me to explain.

Before I conduct so much as even a single downbeat upon meeting an ensemble for the first time, or start any workshop or lecture, I *always* begin with the following disclaimer. I firmly state that the finest teacher I have ever known had a favorite saying. The simple power of the thought has stayed with me and guided me all my life. He used to say that when it came to music, "No one had a corner on truth." When I was eighteen years old I had no idea what he meant. Now that I have socks that are older than that, I understand.

He was trying to get me to realize there was often no right or wrong in music. It has been and always will be an art as well as a science, with answers that are frequently not black or white, but replete with shades of gray let alone fluorescent orange and brilliant periwinkle. This writing is not meant to pretend that there are correct ways. It is merely a collection of ideas to serve as food for thought. I hope it will be a catalyst for you to feel new feelings, think new thoughts, envision new wonders, and realize the magnificence of you, the teacher. For truly, when it comes to teaching, rehearsing or conducting, "no one has a corner on truth."

Years ago, a statement by United States Congressman Jim Nussle reminded us, using that old adage, "If we always do what we always did, we will always get what we always got." His words then, though about politics, are even more fitting for how we must view our own teaching in terms of assessing what does and doesn't work. It is my hope that this book will give you another way to look at the topics that follow, to think about some things a bit differently, recall a few forgotten ideas, challenge some opinions, affirm your beliefs, and possibly rethink some positions.

That process is how we create new paths, or confirm the effectiveness of old paths to our goals. More importantly, in this way, I hope it allows you to further develop your confidence in, and enjoyment of, music and teaching. The best judges of our teaching are always our students. I believe the bottom line should be what *your* opinion is of *your* results and how *you* got them. If you are pleased with your students' accomplishments, and with what you did to get those accomplishments, that is wonderful. If not, I hope this book will provide you with a few ideas to help you not "always get what you always got."

Lastly, I have always believed that to be a good teacher, one had to be a great student. I'm an okay teacher, but I was, and will always strive to be, a far better student. I try to convince those I teach to gather as much information from as many people and sources as they can. To take it all in. Process it all. Then they can keep what they like and abandon what they dislike. The resulting blend, mixed with their own ideas, becomes *them*. Like a great bottle of red Bordeaux wine, the blend — rather than any one single grape variety — is what makes the wine remarkably good.

The brilliant composer Igor Stravinsky, in conversations with Robert Craft for the book entitled *Dialogues*, stated that thought much more powerfully. Regarding his relationship to great master composers of the past, Stravinsky simply said, "Well, which of us today is not a highly conditioned oyster?" We all take the little bits of matter, seemingly unrelated, from numerous sources, over a great deal of time to make our own best "pearl." I hope you always enjoy the art you love, the students with whom you are entrusted, and the sharing of the cherished knowledge which allows you and them to make your own best pearl.

This book is an example of that concept. It is merely a collection of what I have learned from my teachers and students. In fact, this book contains many quotes from people far more learned than I will ever be. Every effort has been made to correctly attribute those thoughts. Where the author is believed to be unknown, no ascription has been made.

Kind support and encouragement from friends, music teachers and students has given me the momentum needed to put these thoughts in writing. I would also like to express my appreciation to you for reading this book. That you, my colleagues, would do so is a kindness I cannot describe. My appreciation for what each of you does everyday is only matched by my awe for your talents and dedication. On behalf of all of the students you have had, have now, and will have in the future, thank you.

Before moving on, however, I would like to share with you the purpose of this book. It is simple. About fifteen years ago, I started presenting workshops based largely on these chapters. I did so for several reasons, the most important of which was that I saw so many of my music teacher friends who didn't seem to enjoy their "art" as much as they once had. Don't get me wrong, they liked teaching music. They were highly effective and dedicated, but they weren't as madly, intensely, or passionately in love with the art of music. They learned to cherish that art in grade school. It sustained and fulfilled them through high school, college and on into their professional lives as teachers. Somewhere along the way, however, that love affair with their music grew a bit subdued. Not the working with kids. Not the sharing of what they know. But simply, that passionate love of music. My desire is to help us remember the profound power and beauty of our art, and how much we truly love it.

The second reason was to help all of us be even more effective, efficient and expedient. We have all of this stored up knowledge, and the desire to teach it, but we want to get more done, faster and easier. What follows are things to consider as we all assess where our students are, where we want them to be, and how to lead them to that goal. Put succinctly, to help us achieve what we want from our rehearsals.

The third reason was to help lessen frustration. If there is one trait we music teachers share, it is frustration. Think about our progression in life. We spend four years at a university studying and performing great masterworks under the hand of remarkable teacher/conductors. There we attend to every detail and nuance of the music, producing concerts that are powerful statements of technique and expression. After four years, we begin our career as music teachers. There we are at the first rehearsal of our fifth-grade band, confidently standing before those young musicians. Knowledge, skill and dedication are oozing from our every pore. The last sound we have rumbling around in our ears is our last performance with the university wind ensemble playing *Candide* or *Rhosymedre* with powerful intensity.

The moment we have waited for all these years is here. We start our rehearsal with the playing of a concert B flat major scale. As we conduct our first downbeat, what we hear shocks us. What was *that?* All we can think is, "That doesn't sound like my college wind ensemble did." Little wonder we can grow frustrated. It can be easy to feel that the results we want are just out of reach, always a bit elusive. Proper perspective allows us to temper that frustration and maintain a more positive attitude. Frustration is often the desire for the achievement of goals in search of the steps to get there.

Will this book solve, teach or cure anything? Probably not. Will we all agree on every topic? Surely not. But if in reminding us of what we already know it feeds the fire that is our passion for music and teaching, it will have succeeded. ▩

THE 33 P's OF
A WONDERFUL REHEARSAL

This chapter is based on a workshop I have had the pleasure of presenting over the past few years. It is one of my favorites because the person who gets the most out of it every time, is me. It reminds me of the teacher I want to be. The person and the personality that I truly want my students to come to know. It always reminds me of goals I have lost touch with, ideas I have forgotten to use, or convictions I have let slip away. It does, however, have the worst title imaginable. When I decided on the title, I asked my wife for her opinion. She immediately declared that it was the dumbest title ever used. She said that no one would know what I was talking about *or* that they would think it is the softest workshop ever given. Sadly, it took me several days to get that musical pun!

Before first presenting this session, I recall sitting with a group of my graduate students. I was asked what the title was. After describing it, one young lady chimed in and said that she was going to develop one called "The 33 D's." I thought for a moment, then responded that I couldn't come up with thirty-three words that started with the letter D that had to do with rehearsals. She immediately said, "Sure, those *darn* saxes, those *darn* sixteenth notes, those *darn* accents…!" Though I have tried to come up with a better title, I have failed to find one that captures the purpose.

What follows is simply a collection of thoughts. There is nothing new here. You already know and do them. These are the qualities that make you a dedicated, vibrant and sincere educator. They are presented to remind you of the many great things you do every day in rehearsals.

Each of us already does these things in our own way. My only suggestion is to check that it is truly happening the way you think it is by videotaping your rehearsals. So often I will watch a videotape of one of my rehearsals and see that what I thought I had done was not what I truly did. What I wanted to do and was sure I had done was not apparent on the tape. I was certain I did a specific thing, but didn't see it once in that hour rehearsal. By videotaping ourselves we can objectively say, "Yes, I can count seven times in the first twenty minutes of that rehearsal that I used positive reinforcement." That way we know we *are* doing it. Not that we *want* to do it, or *think* we are doing it, but that we actually are doing it. That becomes the true barometer of what we do and how we do it. If you don't videotape yourself, you may be missing out on one of the great joys of teaching. To watch a tape and think, "Why did I say that?" allows me a chance to fix the problem before I repeat it. I can realize that I was so worried about the flute pitch that I missed the fact that two percussionists were in the back dueling with bass drum beaters. Whatever it is, we can assess so much, and make corrections during the very next rehearsal. Our growth and the progress of our students will increase dramatically.

When lawyers are trained, they must study countless hours of actual trials. They study every word and maneuver with the hopes of copying what works and not replicating what fails. That is what we need to do on a regular basis. The benefits of that sometimes-intimidating process are remarkable.

Purpose

Simply, that we should have goals that are clearly defined. I mean this in two ways. The first is that the year's goals are clearly defined, not just that we are going to "work with" the kids five days a week for one hundred eighty days. We must define those goals for the students from the very beginning. What concepts should they learn? "By the end of this year I want them to do the following." We may disagree on what the *that* is. We may disagree on whether that should include sight-reading, or scales, or composition. It doesn't matter to me as much *what* it is, but that we can *document* what it is. Then, as we go along, we can assess whether they are meeting those goals. At the end of a day, week, marking period or year we are able to see where they are in relation to our goals. You can firmly say, "They met my goals." Or, "I fell a bit short here, this is what we need to work on more." The key is that there are clearly defined goals rather than just "winging it" day after day.

I often receive phone calls from teachers asking my opinion of a specific concert program. I always frustrate them by responding that they are asking an unanswerable question. Without knowledge of their goals, there is no way to answer the question of whether the pieces are appropriate. If the pieces aren't what we use to teach those goals, we have no vehicle to accomplish our mission. I liken this to someone walking up to you and asking, "Give me your opinion, I'm thinking of getting an appendectomy." To answer that question you need to know if their appendix is inflamed. If they're having a problem with their liver, an appendectomy isn't going to do a darn thing. So, unless we know what the goals are, we can't match the repertoire or rehearsal techniques to them.

The second part of setting goals, which is just as important, is that the students know what those goals are. So often the rule of thumb is to keep the kids in the dark. Thinking that if they know nothing about what's going on, that's safe. Those students sit in rehearsals wondering why they are doing each task. I can hear them asking themselves why they have just spent the last fifteen minutes doing one measure. If they can't answer why they are doing it, how can they be expected to make it better? So let the kids in on it. Tell them why. I agree that once in a while we have to keep them out of the loop simply because of the difficulty level or complexity of the passage. In those cases we don't want to scare them by saying, "This is the hardest measure you'll ever play in your entire life and that's why I'm going to rehearse it ten times." But, generally, telling them what's going on is a good policy.

Plan

Once we have defined our goals, we should detail the sequence in which concepts should be taught. We can prioritize them so it makes sense for us. Do I want them to understand a dotted eighth note followed by a sixteenth note before I want them to understand triplets? And if I do, does that count as a quarter-note, eighth-note triplet or just a three-eighth-note triplet? Think about that. There is a real justification for that, one way or the other. We have to decide, because the repertoire has to match our goals as we prioritize them. We have to set schedules for the day, for the month, for the year, and indeed, for the entire school music program. This is quite simply making certain you have a detailed, district-wide music curriculum. It is the only way to gain consensus on goals, materials and methodology across grades and areas of study. It is the only way to weather change. Those changes of faculty, as well as changes of students from grade to grade, and area to area of specialization within the music program. This may take many hours of meetings (over vast quantities of coffee) but we need to hash this out and come to agreement as to what will be taught and when. You may feel that certain scales should be learned by eighth grade, while some of your colleagues may feel that other scales would be better. Once it is debated and agreed to, each teacher will know where the students are to be at every stage of their training. This understanding should include concepts, materials, instrumentation and every other aspect of the program. If it is clearly understood that by the eighth grade the band will have two tubas, then all involved know what the expectation is and can meet it accordingly.

To this end, we must ask if we always use a lesson plan. Many say to me that they've taught for so many years that they don't need a lesson plan. They know where they are going. I think there is some truth to that. Though I always respond by saying that I've done this a fair number of years and I still won't walk into a rehearsal without one. Granted, a lot of them are made up of one-word blurbs that only mean something to me. God forbid I died before that rehearsal, in that no one would know what that rehearsal was about. That one word, however, is enough to spark my memory as to what I want to accomplish. I remember seeing one of the world's great orchestras being rehearsed by one of the world's great conductors, and he had a list, a lesson plan if you will. It was a punch-list, no different than you would give a builder doing a project in your home. Do this, then this, then this. It was at that moment I thought, "If it's good enough for him, I think I should do this forever." Again, it could just be a little outline. But I think we have to have something, for if we don't, we are just winging it, and winging it always scares me in that it usually wastes time. Time is one thing we don't *have* to waste. Think about it this way: if we have one hundred students in front of us in a rehearsal and we waste even one minute, the compound effect can be staggering. Multiply that by one hundred, because that's the man-hours lost. If we have five of those wasted minutes in a rehearsal, we have to multiply that one hundred man-hour minutes by five, and right there is five hundred man-hour minutes of wasted time in one rehearsal. Multiply that by a week, let alone a year, and think of the wasted time in rehearsals. Whenever I think of that formula, I am overwhelmed by the magnitude of its power. It makes me ever conscious of every second of time during every rehearsal.

With regard to concepts learned as well as music being performed, I want to have a knowledge of where my students are, where they're going, and how I'm going to get them there. At the end of every rehearsal I go to my office with my lesson plan and check my work. Did I accomplish what I wanted? Did I have to veer from my plan, and if so, how? Curriculum and lesson plans should guide *concepts* to be learned. I think performance music, however, needs a bit of additional attention. Before I start rehearsing a work, I make a chart listing each section of each composition being rehearsed. After each rehearsal I grade where that section is at the moment using a simple A through F scale. That tells me where each section is at any given time. So I can say, for example, every section of piece one is an F. That means it has yet to be sight-read. The first section of piece two is a D, which means the ensemble has only read it. The last section of piece three is a C, meaning it has been "roughed in," while the trio of piece four is a B, telling me it has been worked on in detail. The introduction of piece five, however, is an A, which means it has been worked on in fine detail and polished to performance level. So at any juncture I can look at this chart and vividly see where we are, and where we need to go. I can ask myself: why am I rehearsing the introduction of piece five, when it has been an A, while section two of that work is still a C? By doing this, the next time you ask yourself how the Mozart symphony is going, you won't give the simple answer, "Fine, it's getting better." What does that mean? That may not be enough information. But rather you can clearly state that the Introduction to the first movement is an A, the coda is a C, and the like. I need to know that. That helps me with my prioritization for each rehearsal. I know this sounds a bit crazy to some, but after you try it, you may not want to do it any other way.

Pedagogy

Remember that what we do for a living is an art as well as a science. I believe we dwell too much on the art and not enough on the science, or vice versa, depending upon our temperament. Some spend every moment as if teaching a robotic skill and ignore the art. Those students can play any technical passage with precision, and it sounds like a heartless machine. Others spend all of their time on the emotional art and not enough on the science. Those students ooze emotion but can't go over the break without a major catastrophe. So depending on your personality and what comes naturally to you, you will have to work on the opposite traits. Remember to teach something at every rehearsal. I often ask myself what I actually taught in a rehearsal. Did I just simply get through the pieces? Am I only readying them to play a concert? Specifically, what did I teach? It may be a new term, something about a composer, or an alternate fingering. But what was really learned by the students? I think we also have to remember that simply being able to do something or being exposed to something doesn't necessarily mean that it is learned. Is it truly understood?

I often think of the notion of a bandage versus a cure. Obviously, if it is the day before a concert, and there is a problem that you can solve with a quick fix, that's great. Do it. Bandages are wonderful when you need them, but remember to go back after the concert and teach the concept so that gap in the students' learning doesn't stay with them. I also try to keep in mind that concepts truly learned will transfer to new situations, while bandages usually will not.

The phrase that I always think of when it comes to pedagogy is: "Why is it that there is never enough time to do things right…but always enough time to do them over." I'm convinced that if we took the word *again* out of our vocabulary, we wouldn't speak! "Do that again. Let's try that again." We often repeat something over and over again hoping it will get better. Let's face it: that is so very fatiguing. Haven't we all experienced the frustration of playing in rehearsals, repeating a passage for the seventh time having no idea what's wrong, and getting no direction on how to fix the darn thing? Are we teaching in rehearsals, or are we simply repeating a piece over and over with the hope that it will improve? We don't usually need to it again; we need to try to figure out *what* to teach them to do, to make it better. That, I think, is often the hardest part of our profession.

Possible

By this I mean, is it possible? We need to make certain that what we are asking students to do is possible, realistic, achievable, and appropriate. Do they possess the readiness as well as the mental, physical and emotional maturity to accomplish what we want them to achieve? Asking the average sixth-grade band to perform a level six composition is a lofty goal, however, not one grounded in the realities of readiness and maturity. How often do ensembles perform music that is so far out of reach that failure is the only possible outcome? I am not saying we shouldn't challenge our ensembles, or give them music that at times is a stretch, for certainly that is one way to encourage them to grow. I am saying that a challenge can be a positive experience, but being swamped yields frustration and discouragement.

Posture

Someone once asked me to list the top ten most important things to get a band to sound good. It was very easy. I simply listed them in order on a piece of paper: "posture, posture, posture, posture, posture, posture, posture, posture, posture and lastly posture." It's quite amazing, and I'm convinced of it. Bands, orchestras and choirs that have remarkably good posture usually sound wonderful. I have almost never seen an exception. I have never seen an ensemble with impeccable posture that sounded awful, but I have seen a lot of groups that sound awful that have bad posture. I'm not sure if it's the cure, but it's certainly on the path to it. We all know, whether it's bow arm, breathing, hand position or vocal mechanism, it can't be done well without good posture.

Now, I'm not saying that Phil Smith, of the New York Philharmonic, couldn't play the trumpet with both legs wrapped around the back of his head in a bizarre lotus position strung upside down by his ankles, and not sound better than anyone alive! But the typical seventh-grader is not going to sound good sitting crossed-legged playing the trumpet with his elbows on his knees! It's just not going to happen. We can scream "breathe" a thousand times, but with a student hunched over like that it just isn't in the cards. Never underestimate the power of posture. If I had a dollar for every time I've walked into a rehearsal and slid my hand between a person's back and the back of the chair he or she is resting against, or told someone to uncross his or her legs, I would be a millionaire! Now I'm not sure, in the litigious society in which we now live, I would advise you to do the former, but we can certainly verbally attend to those problems.

Position

I would like to address this in two ways. First, *our* position. Simply put, can they see you? This is one of my bugaboos, and all of my students know it. Think for a moment about the typical placement of the conductor with reference to the band or orchestra. Most often, semi-circular rings of players are wrapped around in front of the conductor with the ends of each ring placing performers at or behind the conductor's sides. I believe this notion of having the conductor placed *in* the group is ludicrous for school-aged ensembles. In that setup, what of me are they to see? I have worked very hard on my conducting over the years, but I can confess that I am not capable of conducting a four-pattern with my posterior! I've tried, I really have, but I can't do it. I am the first to agree that this type of set-up is like singing in the shower for the conductor. It sounds great being engulfed and surrounded with tones swimming around your ears, but a large number of players can't see anything. They so often lose a great deal of the view of your hands and face. Or at the very least get the oddest of perspectives.

I have always believed that the podium should be in front of the ensemble with the ends of our rows starting at imaginary lines, like a radius, at forty-five degree angles from the center of the podium. In this way they still won't *all* get a full frontal view, but it will provide enough of a view to allow them to see most of the front of me, and certainly my hands and face. The area to my sides, where no one sits, I call the dead zone. It's like the Dead Sea; nothing can grow there. I won't put anyone there, because they can't see me. If they can't see me, I can't help them, they can't watch me, and I can't *expect* them to do what I am asking for in my conducting. It might not sound as good as the singing in the shower deal, but it is the only way I can guarantee my ability to physically, non-verbally affect any change in rehearsals. After every presentation I have given of this concept, I always have someone say: "That makes so much sense, but I rehearse a one hundred twenty-five piece band in a room slightly smaller than a sardine can, and there is no room as it is." My response is to do your best. Quite often it is impossible, but sometimes with creative thinking, redesigning rows, changing seating plans, somewhat closer spacing, and imaginative use of the shape of the room it can come close to this ideal. Even just a bit of a better vantage-point for the students will yield enormous benefits. As well, *you* being a bit in front of the ensemble makes it easier to hear. If you have ever had a monitor speaker blasting right at you, then you know how hard it is in that situation to hear anything. A few feet of space between you and that speaker makes a world of difference.

The second part of position is *their* position. We need to constantly reinforce and monitor their position. Whether it is hand position, finger position, arm position, embouchure, bow, jaw, cheeks or the like. Clarinet players with fingers nine feet away from the keys, trumpet players with fingers so far over the valve caps as to almost be playing with the palm of the hand, or triangle players using snare drum sticks; we need to address position and technique. Even if it is simply looking at the players, and pointing to our own fingers as if playing the instrument, or walking over to them and correcting their attempt. We vigilantly need to take note. These are all little things that make for giant impediments to progress that can be fixed relatively easily. These corrections take very little time but will affect enormous change in your rehearsal. We need to constantly watch and listen for these things. If French horn players have hands resting on the top of the bell like it is an armrest, we should hear and see this problem in a flash, and we need to address it every time.

Preparation

We must truly know the score. Kids know when we're "winging it" versus when we make mistakes. Lord knows I've made more than my fair share of mistakes in rehearsals. They are forgiving of mistakes. They are never willing to forgive winging it, nor should they. Some conductors "learn" the score on the podium because they know they can. Whenever I think of this, I recall a wonderful cartoon in which you see a conductor standing in front of an orchestra ready to perform. On the conductor's music stand is a simple piece of white paper with the words, "Fake it." We know that we can always stay two feet ahead. However, that means their progress resembles a leapfrog game with us staying just out in front.

Think how much more progress can result from your *starting* miles ahead of them in preparation, pulling them to you, always staying leagues ahead. When people question the necessity of this for young ensembles, I ask them to try it once. Learn even one work cold. Then go into your rehearsal. It's addictive. You become addicted to being that well prepared, that much in control, and that productive. You will see this enormous growth in these fifth or sixth-graders, realize what you got them to do, and come to the conclusion it is nothing short of amazing. You will realize you knew every problem they had before they even got to that page. You'll know that you got things fixed by getting in their faces before they knew they were having problems. You then come to think if that could happen every day, their rate of progress would be awesome. I liken it to studying for a test. If you go into an exam having not really studied, you hesitantly work to gnaw off every question with fear and trepidation. If you have truly studied, you boldly take the exam and find it refreshing, exciting and strangely enjoyable.

My favorite quote about knowing the score comes from Sun Tzu in the book *The Art of War*. (I'm not trying to compare rehearsals to war, though sometimes it may feel that way!) He states, "Every battle is won before the war." It is so true. If you go into a rehearsal knowing the score cold, I guarantee you that you will win. It is going to be a great rehearsal. It's got to be, the deck is rigged in your favor. We go in winging it, and I will likewise guarantee that we will eventually lose. You, the kids, the ensemble, the whole experience won't be as good. Louis Pasteur summed up score study better than anybody. He had no idea because he was too busy discovering scientific wonders, but he was right on the mark for score study when he said, "...chance favors the prepared mind." If you know the score well, you can then find something in the score and say, "Look at this fantastic thing I found in the score." Conversely, if you are so busy in rehearsal figuring out what meter it's in, you're not in any way going to be ready to recognize the little bits of neat stuff, often the genius the composer gives us, buried in the score waiting to be stumbled upon or discovered. If your mind is prepared, chance will favor it!

Abraham Lincoln once said, "If I was given an axe and was told that I had eight hours to cut down a tree, I would spend six hours sharpening the axe." A conductor who is winging it is spending sixteen hours with a dull axe pounding away for naught, when he or she could spend forty-five minutes with a keenly sharpened axe and get a whole heck of a lot done. Just think about that before you go to your next rehearsal.

Pearl

I believe that in every rehearsal we need to make one beautiful pearl. I use a pearl as my model because it is perfect. It has a perfect beginning, perfect middle and perfect end. It's just this one little thing and it's perfect. In and of itself it isn't much, but it *is* perfect. I believe that when we rehearse, we need to give our students this beacon. It may be one chord, one release, or one measure. It can be something tiny. But it has to be as perfect as we are capable of achieving. If we can make one chord so beautiful that we can stop and say, "Listen, did you hear that? Play it again and listen to that. It's magnificent. It's gorgeous, did you hear how beautiful, resonant, rich and in tune it was?" You can get completely jazzed about it.

That pearl does two things: first, it gives them an example of your expectations. How many of us have played under people where we had no idea what the expectation was? We often begin work on a piece in January for a performance in May. Early on our students don't know how it goes, let alone how good it's supposed to get. But if we can play one measure beautifully early on, it sets the expectation level. The students can then say to themselves, "Wow, the whole thing has to be that good in three months." Now they will know where you are headed. Though some may think this will cause frustration because the goal is then made so vivid, I think the opposite. I think the kids will be less frustrated with the work at hand because they will know what the finished product is to be.

I also think it works to encourage progress. Let's face it, all too often nothing we perform starts to sound good until a few weeks before the concert, especially if we are rehearsing big chunks of a piece over and over rather than small sections with ever-increasing progress. Those pearls give them a feeling of accomplishment early in the process. That feeling builds as the little gems grow in number with every passing rehearsal. If something is beautiful in the first week of rehearsing a piece they can then appreciate the fact that something is in the bag. Accomplishment is then identified in smaller amounts early and often, rather than larger and later. They will know they have a long way to go, but that they have made real, tangible progress. Simply put, we must make something vividly and clearly beautiful.

Peace

Years ago I watched a news program on television during which the principal of a school was interviewed. By every measure, her school went from being one of the worst to one of the best in a very short space of time. During the interview for that program she was asked what the secret was to her success. With blazing eyes and a firm voice she very tersely and powerfully looked at the interviewer and said, "Learning cannot exist in chaos." That is the truth. If our rehearsals are not disciplined and quiet, nothing can get done. Nothing. I once watched a rehearsal during which the students were allowed to be completely free and talkative. The students were so disruptively talkative that the teacher had to yell to be heard. With that, the students yelled louder. The teacher then had to curse to be noticed. This chaotic dueling went on and escalated with every passing moment. When we talked about it, I calmly said, "What's next?" He said, "What do you mean?" I said, "All I can think of is an air-horn, and the problem with that is that once it doesn't work anymore, there is nothing left. They love pushing your buttons." They could sit back and sadly think, "How cool is it that we can get our high school band director to stand there and curse out loud at us?"

He came to realize that if he really wanted to get their goat, he would have to start using a series of techniques to hold a firm, disciplined and quiet rehearsal. If he stopped the screaming match with them it would burst their bubble. It would no longer be fun to get a rise out of the teacher, and they eventually would get down to work. I'm not saying we can't have student interaction or that we need to be mean or so strict that there is no enjoyment, but we need to create a disciplined environment. Someone has to maintain order. I always ask people to remember that the same six letters spell the words *listen* and *silent*. I don't believe that is a coincidence! If they are not silent, they can not listen.

Pace

I believe in a very fast pace. I sometimes like to get to the point where I know people are staying awake just to try to see if they can understand what's coming out of my mouth, and stay up with me. I also think we have to have lots of variations of volume, speed, timbre, inflection, pauses, silence and accentuation. I have worked over the years to develop a generally fast pace because as a player I always found that I paid attention in rehearsal more and the time went by faster. At the end of a fast paced rehearsal often I would think, "It's over already?" Whereas rehearsals with a slow pace brought on almost continuous glances at my watch followed by a deep and mournful sigh. I think a fast pace with almost schizophrenic variation prevents the latter. If that is not part of your nature, that's fine. Some of the best teachers I know have a steady, calm, slow and meditative pace. However, if you are searching for ways to enliven your rehearsals, keep your meditative pace, but every couple of minutes add bursts of invigorated, vibrant and almost frenetic pace. *Change* in pace is even more important than trying for a *fast* pace.

A second aspect of pace is in reference to how we work on the music for a particular performance. It seems to me that many conductors ascribe to the following scenario. It's September, and let's say we are going to prepare five pieces for a concert in December. At the first rehearsal we read all five works by starting at the beginning and playing to the end. At each successive rehearsal, we work a bit on each composition by starting at the beginning and working on that piece for as long as time allows. In that way, we keep making the first section of the work better and often end up neglecting much of the end of the work. By sheer repetition they will know the beginning better than the ending.

I call this the *At The Top Syndrome*, in that we usually start each piece with those instructions. At the performance, the beginning of each work is stellar. However, with each passing section of the piece, the performance becomes weaker. In addition, this type of rehearsing almost demands that all of the works will be at about the same level of performance at any given time, and that the *type* of work done in each rehearsal will be about the same. Examples of the latter would be roughing in the basics of the piece, or fine detail work, or polishing. By this I mean almost all of the rehearsals up to only weeks before the performance will be trudging through the roughing in of new material, while the last few rehearsals before the concert will be (hopefully) all polishing. I think either can be devastatingly boring. In the students' vernacular this would be described as: "The first week, everything stinks; the second week, everything stinks; the third week, everything stinks; the fourth week, everything stinks; ...the seventh week, I can possibly smell 'good' coming, but everything still stinks; ...the tenth week, everything's tolerable; ...the eleventh week, everything's not bad; ...finally, the fourteenth week, everything's awesome!" What a terrible thing to do to people.

To remove that possibility, I keep sections of each work at intentionally different levels of preparation. Using the sections of each work, discussed earlier for a progress grading chart, I design my rehearsals so any given one could be described as follows: today we will be sight-reading the introduction of work one, roughing in the coda of piece two, detailing the trio of work three, polishing fine detail of the third variation of piece four, and running straight through work five for review and a sense of context. This manner provides a variety of types of work in each rehearsal, as well as a sense of progress, in that some sections are very well learned early in the game. This then becomes almost an extension of the notion of a "pearl" described earlier.

Perceive

We need to become better aware of problems. We must work to hear pitch more attentively and sense rhythm problems more acutely. We need to watch kids more so we can defuse discipline problem cells before they spread, or note when someone's lost. Simply, we must be more aware of what's going on in front of us. What's happening in rehearsal? Is Susan crying? Why? Has Sam stopped playing his sax? Are the snare drummers playing a measure ahead? Are the trumpets incorrectly playing muted? Is the chime player using snare drum sticks? Are the sopranos all singing the wrong vowel? Can the trombone player see me with that file cabinet blocking his view? Are the clarinets playing a true dotted eighth note followed by a sixteenth note? We need to listen to and observe what is *really* happening, rather than what we want to see and hear. We also can't be so preoccupied with certain players or certain spots in the music that we don't observe the big picture.

This can be practiced by repeatedly watching videotape of a rehearsal and noting your observations, using a set of ensemble error recognition tapes, or by playing a recording of your ensemble and pretending you are judging it for a contest. Listen and critique. Make yourself better at seeing and hearing what is going on.

Pinpoint

Isolate the material you are going to teach. Break learning and growth down into very small steps. Music is the supreme example to me of the adage that every long journey is made up of thousands of single steps. The more isolated each hurdle is, the more possible and less frustrating the process.

Polish

Years ago on my university's campus we had Shari Lewis as a commencement speaker for the College of Education. I might add that I was puzzled about her being chosen for this accolade which included receiving an honorary doctorate. I was taken by the non-academic nature of what she did. After all, she was a puppeteer and television personality. All I could think of was her little Lambchop wearing a cap and gown! At the ceremony she stood to give her speech. She started speaking, and within ten seconds, the thousands in attendance collectively dropped their jaws. We sat mesmerized, listening to the most remarkable speaker many of us had ever heard. During the speech she discussed the great teachers in her life. I must hasten to mention that after the speech I ran home and told my older sister, a gifted early childhood education specialist, about the speech. I said, "Ann, I just heard the most remarkable speech." She asked by whom, to which I replied, "Shari Lewis." She quickly responded, "Well of course, she's wonderful. You didn't know that?" Then without missing a beat, put as only an older sister could, she said, "Boy, you're dumber than I thought you were!" Indeed. The following is quoted from the remarkable Shari Lewis, whose passing was far too soon.

She said that one of the most influential people in her life was a Roshi, a Zen Buddhist teacher, who said teachers: "Concentrate on polishing your own lantern so that others may follow its light." I listened to those words, and I was changed. How many people don't do anything musical for themselves once they start teaching? We must continue to grow as musicians. Whether it's that we continue to perform, study a new instrument or voice, attend concerts, study new works, take classes, or go to museums. We must constantly make this a lifelong process of getting better at our art. Have you ever finished reading a book one night and noticed that the next morning you had a much better rehearsal? Even if the book had nothing to do with music? And if it was related to music, for the next week you were about the best teacher you ever were, and then it starts to wear off. It's true. I remember the day I finished Pablo Casals' magnificent *The Art of Interpretation*. It was a buzz I kept for three months. If we continue to get better at what we do and enjoy our art more, then our students will grow more, just from the glow of how much we love what we do and how excited we are to share it. Another way of saying the same thing comes from a quote by John Cotton Dana, given to me by a teacher after a session I presented: "Who dares to teach must never cease to learn."

Precise

We need to be precise as to what's wrong, what we want, and what our students can do to get there. Specific information they can act on. My favorite story to illustrate this idea is attributed to Sir Thomas Beecham, however, I have heard the same story attributed to half of the conductors in the world. It is about the player who came up to him at rehearsal and said, "Maestro, I would like to talk to you about rehearsal letter F in the Brahms." In a flash the Maestro screamed, "F…(long pause)…F…(longer pause)…F is everyman. It is the world awakening, it is the essence of all beings at one with each other, it is the soul of our collective destiny…ah F." At which time the player looked at him and said, "Yeah, that's great, now you want that thing loud or soft?" It's so true. Sometimes we get so carried away that the information we give isn't precise enough to mean anything to anyone else. We can't be so subjective as to be meaningless. I'm certainly not saying we can't be illustrative in our speech, and I'm as big a fan of metaphor as anyone, but at a certain point it becomes obtuse.

Positive

We have to use positive reinforcement all of the time! Not just sometimes, all of the time. I'm a firm believer that the greater the teacher,
the more he or she uses positive reinforcement. Not only does it allow us to attend to the basic human desire to be praised, but also it
allows us to do it in a way that doesn't compromise our value system.
We don't have to stop a group that sounds absolutely awful and tell
them it sounds great. It doesn't. If they play a major triad that sounds
like every pitch of a chromatic scale played simultaneously, and we say
it sounds beautiful, they know it doesn't. They know it sounds awful.
It only serves to tell them we won't be truthful about their progress or
quality. We can always find things to use positive reinforcement about:
"Clarinets, your posture is wonderful." "Steve, your hand position is
terrific." "French horns, your sound is beautiful." "The introduction is
breathtakingly pretty." We must truthfully praise those things done
truly well. But equally important is to acknowledge *progress* in any area,
without lying to them. Kids know when they don't sound good, but
positive reinforcement moves us along the achievement path.

We have to be a positive spirit. To paraphrase Virgil, we must always remember the simple phrase, "They can who believe they can."
If you convince the trumpets they can play that lick, they *can* play that
lick. If you convince them you don't believe it's possible, they won't.
Haim Ginott, the renowned writer, put it so very well when he said,
"I've come to the frightening conclusion that I am the decisive element
in the classroom. It is my personal approach that creates the climate.
It is my daily mood that makes the weather. As a teacher I possess a
tremendous power to make a child's life miserable or joyous. I can be
a tool of torture or an instrument of inspiration." Quite possibly, those
are some of the best words to live by I've ever come across.

Pleasant

Do we create an environment that is pleasant? Is it safe and comfortable? Do they have moments of success? Are they free to feel emotion
without fear of ridicule? Do the students sense they can try, confident
in the knowledge they will be told when it is wrong, but that they will
be praised when it is correct? Now before you roll your eyes, if I finish

a rehearsal and there weren't moments of tension where they all were on the edge of their chairs, I would feel I failed. But there have to be some moments where a student can leave the room thinking, "Wow, I had a tear in my eye. I actually felt something really cool."

Pleasurable

Do *you* have fun in rehearsals? Do *they* have fun in rehearsals? I'm convinced that if the first is true, the second will be too. There are a lot of times when my students tell me that I "ought to get a life." I think it's because I seem to have a lot of fun in rehearsals. I have a ball. I do, I really do. To me it's real serious business. I eat it, breathe it, and sleep it. I love it. They are some of the most intense moments in my life. That doesn't mean it's not fun. I want my students to see that hard work can be very enjoyable and that I really love music, not by me telling them so, but by me living it.

Pause

Breaks from intense work are necessary. Intensity is great, I'm a firm believer in it, but there have to be breaks from it. Whether it is a story, a joke, a silence, a run through of a section of a work, something to break the monotony and redundancy of relentless, intense work. My favorite story about the need for a break of this kind comes from the first time I conducted the Connecticut All-State Band. One hundred and sixty-one of us were packed into a rehearsal room which eventually grew to be hotter than the surface of the sun. On the side of the room were several sets of double doors leading outside. We kept them open at all times. For three days they rehearsed with incredible focus while being as quiet and behaved as any group in history. During some very intense work at the morning rehearsal of the third day, all of a sudden there was a giant, violent crack of lightning and thunder instantly followed by a torrential downpour. As I continued to rehearse, the students started to laugh. The students held it in until it boiled over and spread from student to student like a virus. Within a flash they were all laughing uncontrollably. At that moment I had to make a decision as to what to do. My first thought, I must admit was, "These kids have been so well behaved for three days, and now they are going to sit there and laugh!" Then I realized they had been working so intensely that they obviously needed it. They needed to collectively "lose it." By then the virus had gotten to me. It was so infectious that people were falling over and holding their sides. I was laughing so hard that I pulled a muscle in my ribcage. After a minute or two, as the laughter had simmered down to a dull, out-of-breath sighing, I asked them what we were laughing at. Through tears of laughter they answered, "We have no idea!" After about another twenty seconds, the laughter stopped as fast as it started, and we went right back to work. The rest of that rehearsal was probably our best. They needed it. Why? I have no idea.

People who watch my rehearsals wonder why anyone who tells jokes as poorly as I do would ever tell a joke in public. Or why I tell my dumb stories or anecdotes. They aren't very good, but they are designed to give that momentary pause when needed. When I have pressed them as far as I think I can press them, I will often back away for a minute and let them laugh, or giggle, or sit quietly, or make fun of one of my stupid jokes.

Pass

There is always a time when we have to just let go. We have to change our course so on that occasion we steer away from the intense challenges of the "rapids" to find enjoyment, fulfillment and unnoticed beauty in the "calm waters" we are in now. Knowing full well that tomorrow, or the tomorrow after that will be a better day to head straight into those rapids. At those times when we decide it isn't going to happen, we need to be willing to simply *pass*. There's always tomorrow or next week. If it's the rainy day before Thanksgiving vacation and it's not happening, let it go. Because we all know that if we push too hard at the wrong time, the damage done could take us three weeks to undo. Just let it go. Run through a section of a piece, do some sight-reading, do some improvisation exercises. I'm not saying to let chaos run rampant, but we may need to back off some on our expectation for that session.

People

No matter what we do in rehearsals, or how we do it, we have to always remember they're people. They may be young or old. They may be seasoned or inexperienced. They may be sharp as a tack or need a bit more time. But they are people. They don't belong to us. Nor will they stay with us. We just have to make certain they will be all the better for the time we share together as human beings. There is a time when what we know matters little, who we have been is meaningless, what we have accomplished is insignificant and what talents we possess are unimportant. That time is when we are looking at those faces in rehearsals and classes. Those human beings who have entrusted themselves to us. I believe they are much less concerned about our past accolades than they are about whether we care about them. I'm certainly not saying we have to be warm and fuzzy all the time. Or that they shouldn't know when we are displeased, but we need to respect them as we wish them to respect us.

This was brought home to me so very powerfully by an experience when I was a college student. During a concert in which I happened to be playing principal trumpet, I had a solo in a work. At the end of the piece our conductor motioned several students to stand who had played solos. I was not one of them. I was crushed. It really bothered me, but I decided to let it go rather than approach the director. At the end of the evening I went back to my dorm and heard that solo over again in my head some three thousand times. I couldn't figure out what I did that was so awful. The next morning, as I opened my mailbox in the music school, I saw an envelope. Upon opening it I saw that it was a handwritten letter from my conductor apologizing profusely for having forgotten me after that composition. He said he had realized it after the concert but could not find me. All I could think was that he cared enough about me as a person to take the time to write that letter. The mere fact that he took the time to *think* of the oversight was amazing. That he would *write* to me was nothing short of genuine concern. Of all that he taught me, all the repertoire and all the techniques, what I remember best is that he cared. He has long since retired, but I still have that note.

Pep-talk

We always need to bolster their confidence. We need to be the one to instill determination. We have to be the one to build their enthusiasm. They can't always do it themselves. We have to help them do it. We must be the catalyst. They can come on board once we have the train moving. But they need our help. Often I wonder if we music teachers weren't all cheerleaders in another life? We all know sometimes that's what it takes.

Passage

We can't work so much on detail we forget to put the whole passage in context. It's what I call the *Letter Q Syndrome*. We work so hard on letter Q, starting every rehearsal at that spot. We work the rhythm, pitch and dynamics over and over again. Can't you just hear it? After the ninety-seventh time at Q, "Let's start at our favorite spot, letter Q." But the night of the concert, if we don't guard against this syndrome, where is the problem? It isn't letter Q; it is the few measures before Q. They know Q better than the back of their hands; they just don't know how to get to Q in context.

I learned this best from my father who loved to fly small airplanes. He was a wonderful pilot. I had always wanted to get my license. When I started training, I didn't tell him. I wanted to surprise him. So after I got my license, I called him from my home in Connecticut and asked him to meet me for lunch at the North Philadelphia Airport. That Saturday, with my dad on the field, I flew in with the best landing of my life. I then pulled the plane over to the parking area from where my dad was proudly watching. I walked over to get a great big congratulatory hug. Then, after we discussed his surprise, we went into the airport for lunch. After lunch, we went to the airplane to take a ride. He asked whether I wanted to do the preflight inspection or should he. I confidently said that I would. In an effort to convince my dad, who was the best pilot I had ever known, that I really knew what I was doing, I proceeded to give that airplane the most thorough, detailed and focused preflight in the history of aviation.

I checked every screw. I knew every rivet by name. I'm pretty convinced I could have given you the social security number of the person who tightened every bolt and what he ate for breakfast on the day he did it! I checked every detail as if with a magnifying glass. My father stood and watched every moment. At the end, I called over to him and said, "All done, let's go." His response: "Hell no, I'm not getting in that deathtrap!" He went on to say that I wasn't done. I stood there trying to figure out what I had missed. What detail had I neglected? He then walked away from the plane and stood looking at its nose. I walked over and stood next to him. He then asked if I was "looking at the plane." I said, "Yes." He asked if I was "really looking at the whole airplane." I said, "Yes." He then said, "Now you're done." As we walked to the plane, I asked him to explain the lesson he undoubtedly was trying to teach me. He feared I was so preoccupied by the minutia of the details, looking in such a myopic way, that I would miss the big picture: the bent wing or leak on the ground, only seen with the perspective provided by distance. He said, "You were so worried about the rivets and screws that it could have been the wrong airplane and you wouldn't have noticed it." So for us, we always need to look at the big picture of the piece. The seams getting us to and from a section are as important as the section itself. Dad would like that.

Past

Make sure that we always review what has been learned. I constantly remind myself of the incredible truth found in the phrase, "We need be taught much less than we need be reminded."

Push

We always have to press them to be ever better. Constantly raising the bar. They need to know that the second they get over the bar, it is instantly three inches higher. The expectation is that they will constantly try their hardest to improve bit by bit. The bits may be small, but always better. The story I tell every ensemble with which I have ever worked is about a time I was conducting in a very poor region of this country. It was one of the poorest areas I had ever been in. I was rehearsing in the "cafe-gymna-bandroom-natorium," which was affectionately called "the room." It was the only large room they had. We spent several days working very hard. They were wonderful students and played incredibly well. They were, however, from humble means. They were playing on instruments being held together with duct tape that I would have made into a planter years before. They had little if one measures by earthly possessions. Just before the concert, they taught me what *they had* that was far greater. I was told to wait in the hall outside of the cafe-gymna-bandroom-natorium to be announced for the start of the performance.

I stood quietly listening to my introduction. As I did, I happened to look up above the door leading into the room and saw a small wooden plaque where someone had etched in the following words with a pen: "Today I will give everything I have, for anything I keep I will have lost forever." I stood there as tears filled my eyes. I heard my name announced. I heard the applause, but I couldn't move. Finally, my host came over to the door and asked if I was ready. Seeing the tears, he asked if I was okay. I replied that I just needed a minute. I was absolutely dumbfounded. Those people had the integrity, work ethic, and dedication to publicly state they weren't going to waste one minute. They weren't going to make it good for the night of the concert. They were going to try their hardest to make it good every time, right then and there. They realized that any opportunity they had, but missed, to make it better, was lost forever. I try to think of that every time I walk into a rehearsal thinking it's just going to be a rehearsal. It isn't just the next forty-five minutes. It is the only time those forty-five minutes will exist. Those dedicated and talented students and teachers knew. They taught me more that day than they ever could have known. As W. Somerset Maugham reminds us, "It is a funny thing about life: If you refuse to accept anything but the best, you often get it."

Persevere

We must continue the course no matter what. No matter the difficulty. No matter the opposition. No matter the frustration. We can't get discouraged. I'm not saying that we have to be so rigid with our plans as not to take those unexpected detours of creative teaching which are often our best moments, or at times we can't take that "pass" on our goal for the day. I'm talking about the big picture. The path you want students to take to get to where you know you are going. That place where you can step back, listen to what they have achieved, realize what *you* have given them, realize what *they* have given you, and more importantly realize what they have given *themselves*. It will happen. They will get there. It may take a bit longer than any of us would like, but if we stay the course, it is going to happen. Marilyn vos Savant was so very correct when she said, "Being defeated is only a temporary condition, giving up is what makes it permanent."

Praise

We all know we must constantly reward achievement. Human nature being what it is, we all want that pat on the back. The problem we often find ourselves in is that we either have to wait until something sounds great to reward it, or we have to lie and say it is great when it isn't. If we wait until it is all perfect we obviously will be praising them sometime in the next millenium, for I believe there is no such thing as perfect in art. If we lie, they will probably know it and then ignore all future praise, assuming it too is a lie, or they will believe us and develop such low expectations that we will never convince them of the goals ahead. The only way out is to break our achievement objectives into such small amounts — such tiny steps — as to allow them to achieve great results on a regular basis. That gives us the opportunity to truthfully praise real results frequently. But how do we instill a sense of appreciation and reward for results that are getting better, but are still not very good? I used to teach with a wonderful gentleman who always reminded his students to "praise approximation." I hated that thought! I wrestled with that sentiment in my mind until I was exhausted. It truly bothered me. Then I realized our disagreement was semantic in nature. I took the word "praise" in his mantra to mean that if the achievement was even approximately correct we should tell them it was great. What he meant was that we have to acknowledge and reward the fact that the results are getting ever closer to the goal. Quite simply we have to be encouraging along the way rather than wait until a goal is truly *reached*. Just remember that the same letters that make the word *praise* are used to make the word *aspire*. If we don't praise them, they will not aspire. We don't have to wait until it's perfect to help them know it's getting better.

The 33P's of a Wonderful Rehearsal

Pride

They need to be proud of their accomplishments from you praising them, and from them sensing their success. They need to know when you are happy and pleased with their progress or achievements. True, our goal should be that they sense personal fulfillment from within, however, we have to show them how proud we are of them along the way. Adapting that well-known maxim, "We must help them to take pride in how far they have come, and to have faith in how far they can go."

Plant

We have to remember that we are not conducting the New York Philharmonic. We're not even conductors or teachers. You know what we are? We're farmers. We plant seeds. We plant seeds that we may never see come to complete fruition. That's what we do. It is sometimes hard to remember that. We can't get frustrated or try to tackle too much now because we are planting seeds for the next month, the next year, the next generation, for time to come. Don't think that just because they "didn't get it" now, they won't someday "get it." You may be wondering why I chose to use the word plant in this chapter rather than the word patience. I did so because to me, planting, with the above connotation, is the ultimate in patience. I often think of patience as being sought for the moment, as opposed to planting, which implies holding one's patience for a very long germination.

Perspective

Keep it all in perspective: the moment, the rehearsal, and the year. Remember what's really important: that they love and appreciate music, themselves and their world. With your guidance, patience and example, they will.

Productive

Do *you* and do *they* feel the goals with which we started this chapter have been accomplished? Because if you don't, or they don't, something is wrong in the process.

Passion

We have to have and show this most contagious of things called passion. Jim Elliot once wrote, "He is no fool who gives what he cannot keep to gain what he cannot lose." You can give as much passion as you want in rehearsals and it will never deplete your supply, for you were not destined to keep that. The joy of them experiencing passion, however, can never be taken away. The looks on their faces, the tears in their eyes when you know they have experienced passion, is a gift for all time that you can never lose.

Years ago after a concert, I went on stage to gather my belongings, and was standing on the podium when my wind ensemble string bass player walked up to me. He actually waddled. You know the famous string bass waddle that looks somewhat like the lumbering of an intoxicated elephant. He got as close as he could to the podium and said, "Dr. Boonshaft, could I speak with you for a moment?" I said, "Surely." He said, "Do you know rehearsal letter C in the Boysen we performed tonight?" I said, "Yes." To which he very calmly and professionally said, "I happened to be looking at you at that moment, and I am pretty convinced that you were possessed by the devil himself." I said, "How so?" He said, "Well, I looked up and the face that I saw was like the following." Whereby he proceeded to make a face that would have scared Frankenstein. He then said, "I'm pretty sure no human being would naturally do that, so it had to be the devil." Then with a knowing grin he turned and waddled away. The moral of that story to me is that we can never be afraid to show emotion. It will be seen and appreciated even if we don't know it.

Potential

Never underestimate their potential or your potential. As the saying goes, "Kids can do anything, we just have to show them how." According to Anatole France, "To accomplish great things, we must not only act, but also dream; not only plan, but also believe." We can follow the advice of the remarkable sentiment: "To achieve all that is possible, we must attempt the impossible. To be as much as we can be, we must dream of being more."

Powerful

Never lose sight of the power of what we do. It never ceases to amaze me how overwhelming it is. We help people express their emotions and feelings. That is our job. We teach people to cry. We help people to experience heights of excitement they have never known. We have the ability to touch people's souls. We can change their lives.

Years ago, before a final concert for the year, I was given a poem by a third clarinet player in my ensemble. After the concert I sat in the green room and read it. As I read her words, tears streamed down my face. The poem hangs framed on the wall in my office just behind the music stand where I practice my conducting. It is positioned so that all I have to do when I get frustrated and decide I should give up is to turn around and it is right at eye level staring at me. Suffice it to say it seems I read it about ten times a day! It has gotten me through the best and worst of times. It is not coincidence that you will notice many of her words present in the preceding pages.

Though it was given to me, it is really a gift meant for all music teachers. I just happen to be the caretaker. All of your students have either said or thought the same things about you. They might not have taken the time to write them down, or they may be too shy to show them to you if they had, but this is what every single student in your ensembles, lessons and classes thinks, has thought and will think. This is how important what you do is in the life of a child. Even if they don't know these words, this is what they want to say to you:

"I catch your eye
and hold it,
hold it for an eternity.
Your eyes
    scream with excitement,
            anger,
            pride,
            satisfaction,
            exhilaration.
Your eyes
    speak of love,
        concern,
        understanding.
Your eyes
    cry with a strong desire,
      a desperate yearning,
      to help us reach
      our full potentials,
      our goals.
You care—
    I can see it in your eyes."

The next time you get frustrated or wonder what this is all really about, remember that third clarinet player. Remember that your students are looking right at your eyes and into your heart and soul.

COMMON
MISUNDERSTANDINGS
IN CONDUCTING

Many years ago a dear friend asked me to develop a workshop for a convention of music educators. It was to incorporate ideas he had seen me use in various conducting classes. I was thrilled. I decided the title of the session would be "Thoughts on Conducting." I wanted a title that reflected my hope for the session, namely, to have people simply *think* about how and why they conduct. A self-assessment, if you will. I was convinced that title was sound. Well, months later I saw a flyer advertising the convention with my session entitled "Errors in Conducting." After pulling myself up from the floor, getting over third degree shock, and re-reading that flyer twelve times, I called my friend. When I inquired about the "new" title, he said that in his opinion it much more accurately stated the purpose. I fervently replied that I felt no one had the right to say something was *wrong* in conducting. After great debate, with me on the losing end, the new title went forward.

On the day of my session, at the appointed hour, I walked into a room full of people. Though I was delighted so many wanted to hear the session, I was petrified that from that title they would all think me to be the most egotistical person on the planet. I started the session by apologizing for the superciliousness of the title. Throughout the session I must have repeated that apology twenty times! I didn't want them to think in any way the purpose of the session was to point out what we do that is "wrong," but rather to *think* about what we do, or think about it in a different light.

At the end of that session I was asked to present it again at four different conferences. In the weeks following that conference, I received even more requests to do the same. I was extremely shocked and flattered that anyone would want to listen to anything I had to say, but what happened next baffled me even more.

For each of those subsequent conferences, I was asked to send in a form with the title and description of my session. "Thoughts on Conducting," my *I'm-not-trying-to-tell-you-what's-right, only-some-ideas-to-think-about* title, was sent in. Each time I did, I received a phone call saying, "No, that isn't the session we want. We want that one on "the *errors* we all make in conducting." *Now* it wasn't my original title, or even the revised title of the first presentation. With time it had mutated to one that was even worse! I kept sending them the original title, and they kept changing it to the one *they* "wanted." After having that conversation several times, as well as arriving at conferences only to see the "Errors" title on the program without my even knowing it, I gave up. So I added the word "misunderstandings," kept the awful word "errors," and from that day on, the session has been known, I am sad to say, by the title "Common Errors and Misunderstandings in Conducting."

This chapter is *not* about errors. It is about misunderstandings. True, we may be arguing semantics, but I believe there is a difference. To me, an error is something we do intentionally or unintentionally that is blatantly "wrong" in someone's opinion. A misunderstanding is something we do intentionally, usually out of habit, that doesn't get us the desired result, but we haven't really thought about why we do it that way. As well, a misunderstanding can be something we do intentionally that we *have* thought through, but that doesn't work because our logic or reasoning for using it is flawed.

The purpose of this chapter is simply to get us to think about *what* we do, *how* we do it and *why* we do it that way. And most importantly, whether it gets us the desired results in the most efficient manner. Simply put, I want to be able to say I have thought about what I do, and have confirmed it is what I want to be doing. If we do something intentionally, after assessing the logic for its use and effectiveness, we can confirm it to be what we want to be doing. At that point, I believe we have done what we need to do. We may disagree about the *what*. We may argue about the *how*. But for each of us, after we go through that thought process, it would be what *we* believe to be the *best* way. Again, I don't think there can be a right or wrong way when it comes to music, especially with regard to teaching and conducting.

If I intentionally do a gesture, and it fails to get me the desired result, you may call that an error. I wouldn't. I would call that a misunderstanding. If I did that gesture, and it didn't work, then I must have misunderstood the logic or reasoning behind why or how that gesture should have been used. I apply a simple test to each thought in this chapter discussing various gestures of that mystical communication we call conducting. I ask myself if I can say, "Yes, I do that gesture intentionally and it works to get the result I want efficiently and clearly." If I can say that, it is correct for me. You may hate it! But that's why we have scads of different flavors of ice cream. If however I say, "Yes, I do that and maybe I'm not getting the results I want from it." Or, "Yes, I do that and I'm not sure why." Or, "Hmm, I didn't realize I do that and I don't want to be doing that." Then I might want to think about why I do it and whether I should change it to something else.

The following pages will only address conducting technique and the logic behind its use. Though it is virtually impossible to separate that skill from all of the other attributes necessary to be a wonderful teacher, for our purposes here, we will. If you think the purpose of this chapter is anything more than to give you things to think about, then I have failed. It is simply here to offer food for thought. If, however, after reading these words, you can reflect on what you do, and assess whether it is the way you want to be doing it, then I will have succeeded. That is true even if you disagree with every word of every page. My sole hope is to help each of us *allow* our conducting to help us be more effective and less frustrated, so we may enjoy our art more, and better help students discover the beauty and power of music.

We *will* undoubtedly disagree about a lot of what follows. I think that is wonderful. Creative disagreement is what makes us challenge our deeply held beliefs. We may alter them or come to value them even more, but that process is how we constantly improve. There is one thing about conducting, however, on which we will have to agree. Whether we like it or not, conducting is in great part how we as music teachers are judged. Think about it. How many times have the parents of your students observed you giving lessons? How often does the school board see you teach a class? When was the last time the administration watched you tutor a soloist or coach a chamber ensemble? Never? Probably rarely. Many of those constituencies have arrived at their entire opinion of your teaching abilities based solely on the performances you have conducted. With that said, let's look at conducting as we know it.

The Traditional Approach

For the purpose of this discussion, I am going to lump together what has, by and large, been handed down to us as conducting. Let's call it the traditional approach. Though there are a myriad of different opinions about this wonderful skill, I am basically going to make a "stereotypical average" so as to have a starting point. We will be speaking in broad generalities, but we can nonetheless describe a great number of characteristics shared by many conductors.

MODEST AMOUNTS OF TRAINING

The first generality, and one that I am sure we can agree on, is that music teachers are given only a modest amount of training in conducting. Think about all of the classes you had in undergraduate school. How many ear-training classes did you have? How many music theory or foreign language or piano classes? Now think about how many conducting classes you had. I bet in many cases we may be talking about a three-to-one ratio. In many states the number of credits in conducting required to become certified to teach music is frighteningly few. Please don't think for a minute I am saying those other courses are not enormously important. We all know they are. However, if conducting is as important as I believe it to be for effective teaching and to how we are judged, those few courses are simply not enough.

Some years ago, I took an informal survey of experienced music teachers. I asked them to list the areas in which they felt weakest as teachers. Almost seventy-five percent of them had conducting as number one, and virtually all of them had it somewhere on their list. So, armed with the notion that conducting is extremely important to our success and thereby to the success of our students, and that most of us feel we have not had as much training as we should, what happens as we evolve as conductors?

TRIAL AND ERROR

Though some of us go on to the advanced study of conducting with a fervent passion, I believe most of us learn a great deal of our conducting by trial and error. We go in front of our ensemble for the first time. We try a gesture. If it works, we think, "Great, now I'll put that in my permanent bag of tricks." However, if it doesn't work, we often panic and then try something else. We do that over and over again until we find something that is successful. That is so time-consuming, but worse, so very frustrating for all involved. Those "arrived at" gestures then become habits. Possibly good habits, but more often than not if we don't go back and correct the root of the original problem, we allow those gestures to become bad habits. If each succeeding step in the process of arriving at a "successful" gesture takes us farther along a path that contributes to communication problems, such as over-conducting, counting off, or multiple preparations, we have made matters worse.

Think about it this way. You have just finished your very modest amount of training in the skill of lion taming. The first time you walk into the lion's cage, you remember to look right at the lion and say, "Nice lion — stay." Well, despite the best efforts of your lion-taming professor, that lion bites you on the backside as you run screaming. Are you likely to try that technique again? Even if you know it *can* work, because it worked for your teacher, will you go back in the cage and try it for a second time? Heck no, if you're anything like me, you'll grab for the nearest whip and chair! Then if the whip and chair fails…(well, you get the point).

The same holds true for conducting. If our first downbeat fails to get our desired result, we may not *calmly* assess the problem. We may grab for that "whip and chair" by using multiple preparations. Then if that fails, we may go to counting off. Once we see those "solutions" work, we will not be inclined to go back to other gestures, even if we feel they are more appropriate. Once bitten by the lion, who would want to try that technique of saying "stay" ever again?

ANYTHING WORKS

The next thing I hope we can agree upon is that when it comes to conducting, anything works. Anything! With enough rehearsal time for vast amounts of repetition, any gesture can be made to work. To prove that point, when I have a group of people at a session, I often run a short rehearsal. My "performers" are taught that every time I tap the top of my head I want them to slow down. When I hit my chest I want them to speed up. If I strike my right knee I want a more legato articulation, but if I hit my left knee I want them to get softer. Stamping my right foot on the floor means marcato, while tapping the sole of my left shoe is staccato. The crowning gesture in my rehearsal is the instruction for them to stop when I hit my bottom. With great detail they practice performing with me using those gestures to "conduct" them. Eventually it works. I *can* run a rehearsal using those gestures. I look like an angry mule or itchy orangutan doing it, but it works.

It does not, however, provide an *internally consistent* foundation on which we can convey additional layers of information. It is not transferable to any other situation and we end up wasting enormous amounts of time. I hope another point we can agree on is that time is one thing we *don't have* to waste. It is surely our worst enemy.

A METHODOLOGY

If so much of our conducting is developed through trial and error, is it then learned as a series of random movements, rather than a systematic approach to learning a language? If so, there won't be a methodology to train players to understand conducting as a nonverbal language. Think of it in terms of learning a foreign language for the first time. Let's say I am going to teach you French. You have the option of signing up for one of two different approaches.

Choice A will have us meet daily for two months of classes here in America, during which time I will teach you vocabulary words. You know: this is the word for dog, hospital, bathroom, bakery, hotel, bus, medicine, police officer, bank, and the like. Each day I will teach you those words, have you practice them, and not move on until the vast majority of you understand their meaning and use. Then after those months of training I am going to fly you to France, drop you off in downtown Paris and say, "Learn how to speak French. I will pick you up in a month." At the moment I would walk away from you in Paris, think about the feeling you would have in the pit of your stomach: pretty excited, right? Maybe a bit worried, but optimistic and eager. You know that you have a basic knowledge of what many words mean.

Choice B has me meet you on the first day of class, at that moment fly you to France, and drop you off in downtown Paris with the same instructions. Now, not speaking a single word of French, what would you feel in the pit of your stomach? I would be crazed with fear and trepidation. I would only be able to think, "I don't know how to ask about the location of my hotel, I don't know the word for bathroom, or anything else. I can't speak a single word of French, and I have to learn it here in downtown Paris while everything else is going on." You *will* learn French in that way. But I can't imagine it would be the least bit enjoyable. I sincerely question whether the amount of time needed for that approach, or the anxiety and frustration levels created, would be worth it. It seems logical to me that it would be easier to learn how to read, write and say vocabulary words in French before we try to create long sentences and stories.

REPETITION

Many years ago, during a session at a convention on this topic, a woman raised her hand and said, "I think this is a neat idea. I have never thought to teach my students to understand my conducting as a language. But I have a question: why do my kids finally 'get it' by about the seventh time?" "That's easy," I replied. She said, "It's that they're stupid, right?" I said, "Heck no, your kids are brilliant!" She looked at me like I was crazy. I continued by saying, "Only seven times? That's wonderful!" With a truly puzzled look on her face she said, "Would you please explain that?" I went on to say that so often we repeat a passage over and over, offering instructions each time along the way. Even if we just beat time, our students will often "get it" by about the fifth, sixth or seventh time. *Why* do they then "get it?" Actually, the question would be better put *how* do they then "get it?"

Here's the way it often goes in rehearsal, if our conducting isn't communicative enough: "Ladies and gentleman, let's start at the beginning." We play through the first section of the work. Then the trumpets miss a crescendo in measure forty. (They were playing with that "dynamics optional" approach!) We then exclaim, "Trumpets, measure forty, there's a crescendo." We play it a second time. Again, they miss the crescendo. (This time they look at us with that "who us, you must be incorrect" look only trumpet players can muster.) "Trumpets, you missed it again," we say. "In measure thirty-nine the oboe begins to play the melody, then in the next measure you have a crescendo." Now on this, the third playing, some sharp students play the crescendo, but not many. "Trumpets, please think. In measure thirty-eight there is a cymbal crash, at measure thirty-nine the oboe begins to play the melody, and then in measure forty you have a crescendo."

On the fourth playing it is better because some of the trumpets took note of the cymbal crash, but it is still not close to good. Now more heatedly you say, "Trumpets, look, in measure thirty-seven the percussion come in, at measure thirty-eight there is a cymbal crash, at measure thirty-nine the oboe begins to play the melody, and then in measure forty you have a crescendo." On this, the fifth playing, though still not executing the crescendo, the trumpets start to really listen for the percussion entrance, the cymbal crash and the oboe. "Trumpets, we can do better! In measure thirty-six there is an accent in the tubas, in measure thirty-seven the percussion come in, at measure thirty-eight there is a cymbal crash, at measure thirty-nine the oboe begins to play the melody, and then in measure forty you have that crescendo."

At this point, the trumpets are learning the stream of events leading to their crescendo, but just don't have it yet. Even if we don't *tell* them these clues, they start to pick them up with each repetition. After playing it for the sixth time, in frustration we say, "Trumpets, look, in measure thirty-five the clarinets enter. Then in measure thirty-six there is an accent in the tubas, in measure thirty-seven the percussion come in, at measure thirty-eight there is a cymbal crash, at measure thirty-nine the oboe begins to play the melody, and then in measure forty you have a crescendo!" Getting ready for playing number seven, the trumpets realize the design of the piece. As they play through the work this time, with knowing looks on their faces, you can just imagine them saying to themselves silently, "There's the clarinet, now the tuba accent, that's percussion, there is the cymbal, I hear oboe melody — get ready — crescendo *now!*" They get it! "Now, that was perfect," we declare. The truth is that our students are brilliant. In that situation, they manage to memorize the events of a work well enough to use them as guides to when and how they play. When you think about it that way, I said to the woman, "Your kids aren't stupid, they're dazzling." If they have not learned to read and understand their conductor's nonverbal language of the hands, they must learn a work by repetition and memory. Though it works, it again requires so much time. This scenario can be especially true when what is desired is not printed in the music, or is not indicated clearly.

SHOWING VERSUS CAUSING

In addition to what has already been stated, often conducting gestures are used to show when something is supposed to happen. If our con-

ducting motions show an event for the players *as it happens*, it is probably too late to be useful to them. Reaction time is needed for players to
see a gesture, decipher its meaning, decide on a course of action, and
physically act upon it. That's why we have yellow lights on traffic signals. Have you ever driven in places where they only have green and
red on their lights? The light goes from green to red with absolutely
no warning. Suffice it to say that is not the most relaxing method.
Now picture driving along on a road. You see a green light ahead. As
it changes to yellow you think, "Ah, yellow, I better get ready to stop."
No panic, just plenty of time to react.

Due to reaction time, if we conduct a gesture when it is to "sound"
it will be late at best. To remedy that, we can *cause* the result we want
to happen before it is needed. If there is to be a subito-piano on the
down beat of measure twelve, we must physically represent it before
that beat so they have time to react to the gesture before the result is
needed. When gestures are seen in advance of their necessity, allowing
time to calmly act upon them, players seem more relaxed and confident. I like that. Calm is good.

THE EVOLUTION OF CONDUCTING

Over the years of thinking about conducting, I have often wondered
how we arrived at this point. How did conducting evolve? I don't mean
the history. I question more the process of how we inherited the art,
and how it has been applied to music education. Why is it perceived
the way it is? Our current way of conducting is relatively young as
music goes. Certainly, its precursors have existed for as long as man
has made sound. However, it really has been only since we managed
to get the keyboard to the back of the orchestra (said with the deepest
respect and admiration for keyboard players) that conducting, as we
now know it, has existed.

Once that happened, we needed someone to lead all aspects of the
performance, not from the keyboard or concertmaster's chair but from
center stage. But who? Can't you just imagine the concertmaster (or
someone of that caliber), the former keyboardist or the composer being perfect? It is easy for me to envision those great musicians leading
the best forces they could gather. And we could certainly argue how
much those players needed gestural communication from the conductor as compared to our fifth-grade orchestra. How much of what those
great players did in performance was done because of their genuine

musicianship? The idea of really *teaching* conducting, let alone using conducting *to teach,* is relatively young. In my opinion, the great strides made in the evolution of music education necessitated the development of conducting pedagogy, and the use of conducting in educational practice. We all owe as much to the legendary *teachers* of conducting as we do to the renowned conductors themselves.

Tradition has undoubtedly played a great role in the evolution of conducting. Much of what we do as conductors has been handed down from generation to generation like the performance practice of percussion playing in Sousa marches for the U.S. Marine Corps Band. Though I respect tradition as much as anyone, I think we also need to view our conducting with the words of Paul Creston when he wrote, "One must distinguish that which is traditional because it is right from that which is right only because it is traditional." Truer words have never been spoken. I wouldn't want to dismiss an idea simply because it is new, nor would I ever want to blindly accept an idea because it is traditional. Both require assessment based on effectiveness and applicability.

As we assess our own conducting, we need to think of Einstein's often quoted definition of insanity: "Doing the same thing over and over again and expecting a different result." If we continue to make gestures that don't get us the desired result, it is doubtful that continuing to make them will ever yield a better outcome.

What Do We Want From Our Conducting?

As we start this assessment of communication from the hands and face, it may be helpful to think about what we hope to achieve through their use. Why do we do it? I posed that question to an experienced music teacher once, and his only reply (after looking completely dumbstruck) was that he had passed that course in college. Interesting question, isn't it? I think it is like asking why we eat, breathe or sleep.

WHAT IS THE GOAL?
Many years ago after a concert I had conducted, a person in the audience came up to me and asked, "What is the greatest compliment someone could give a conductor?" Well, at that moment my conductatorial ego went crazy! Thoughts of: "A holiday on my birthday? A building named after me? A statue in a nice garden?" Then (arriving

back on planet Earth) I said, "That he or she had control." She replied, "That's it? That's the best compliment?" To which I said, "Yes, that's it." Looking puzzled she said, "Not that it made me cry, or gave me chills, or said something to my soul? Why?" I said because control *is*, or *is not*. Everything else is really just opinion.

I went on to explain that if I conduct a phrase a certain way, and you find it harsh, sterile or otherwise distasteful, you would say my conducting is bad. But I happened to have liked it that way. That is really a matter of taste. It is a value judgement. If I got them to do that phrase, that's control. That is a fact. Though you may hate my interpretation, question my taste, or feel my understanding of the work is poor, you can't question that I communicated my wishes to the performers.

So how do we get that control? In an effort to detail a method of conducting that was systematic and especially applicable for educational use, I developed what I call *The Proactive Conducting Method*. Over many years, with many patient students, this approach was formed. I am extremely comfortable with it, and many of my students have met with success using it, but it is certainly only *one* way. It just happens to work for me. My purpose here is not to espouse that method. However, I believe the characteristics, attributes and goals of that approach, as with those of many other fine approaches, can help one to gain that control.

WHAT IS THE PURPOSE?

Before describing the qualities we would want to see in any approach to conducting, we need to agree on the purpose of conducting. A definition of sorts. I'm not trying to define the role of a *conductor*; for that we would need the mainframe computer from NASA. I am talking about the purpose of the gestures a conductor uses. I am certain that if we place two hundred conductors in a room, we will have two hundred and one opinions as to that purpose. Be that as it may, we need to come up with one that can serve as a foundation for the pages that follow. What do we really want to accomplish with our conducting? What do we hope to do?

To answer that question, I think we must first agree that conducting is an art as well as a science. The artistry of movement without an understanding of the mechanics and logic of a gesture can lead to an emotional portrayal with little precision. Conversely, conducting that dwells on precise, machine-like movements without the passion and soul of artistic motion will be sterile and lifeless. It is in the balance of conducting, as an art and science, that we find our stride.

As to a definition of the purpose of conducting, I would like to put forth one that will hopefully offend no one. Is it the only answer? No. Is it complete? Absolutely not. Does it include all the aspects of excellent conducting? Positively not. My hope, however, is that it is benign enough that we can agree to its usefulness. Despite its banality, I believe it captures the essence of what we want from conducting gestures. For me, the purpose of conducting is *to emulate sound in motion*. (At this point if we were gathered at a convention session, I would duck down below the lectern and cover my head with my arms. Then, slowly rise up as I look for weapons!) In its simplicity, I find truth. I hope to portray the sounds I come to want from interpreting a score in the motions I make. Though we could go on for pages, I think that is a safe place to find agreement. Do you concur? Can you live with that thought? If so, then you have to agree with the next point.

If you agreed to the usefulness of that statement, then inherent in that definition is that conducting is visual communication. If motions are to "mean" something, then they must be communication of some kind, and if they are physical rather than aural, then they must be visual communication. When thinking about visual communication, I believe we can delineate two types.

The first I will call impressionistic. A perfect example of this would be the canvas of an impressionistic painter. We all have seen those beautiful works that offer us the feeling of the subject. They are often fuzzy in nature, lacking specificity or precision. But in their lack of clarity we are offered the essence or nature of its content. If I compose an impressionistic painting of New York City for you, it will give you the *feeling* of that magnificent place. It will be "New York City*ish*." Will it show you the layout of the streets, the detail of the architecture, or the specifics of the exact location? No, but you will come to sense the vibrancy, perceive the intensity, and savor the pathos.

The other broad type of visual communication is what I call functional communication; that of a language. A great example of that is semaphore. Though I may be dating myself, I remember learning that very detailed, specific and mechanical language of using flags to communicate. Each visual representation of your arms with those flags offers information to those who observe you. It is a wonderful example of movement intended to be functionally communicative. However, the quintessential example is sign language.

Picture me standing in front of you, holding my hand in the air so my fingers are stretched out, extending directly upward with no gaps between them, and my thumb is bent inward pressing on my forward-facing palm. Would that have any meaning to you? Would you know what I'm saying to you? It is the letter B. Try making that shape with your hand. Look at it for a moment. That is a B. You have just learned the letter B in sign language. It's not a big B, a sad B, a majestic B, or a mournful B; it is simply a fact. It gives you exact, clear, specific, dispassionate information.

Now picture me doing that same "gesture" again. Would it have any meaning to you this time? If I saw you in an hour, and made that gesture, would it have meaning to you? How about next week? Next year? I want you to picture me standing in front of you making that gesture once again, but this time I want you to force yourself *not* to think of the letter B when you see that hand sign. Almost impossible, isn't it? That is the power of visual communication that is functional in nature. Through its consistent use, it retains meaning. If tomorrow, however, I teach you that the gesture means the letter Q, it causes confusion. If the next day I teach you that it means the letter K, it ceases to have meaning altogether. It can no longer function as part of a language.

Characteristics of Conducting

To incorporate all of what has been stated previously into an approach to conducting, we can identify six goals or characteristics we would want to include.

COMMUNICATE FUNCTIONAL AND IMPRESSIONISTIC INFORMATION

Our first goal is to use functional and impressionistic visual communication in our conducting. To communicate functional as well as impressionistic nonverbal information. To use conducting to communicate every aspect of what the music demands, and how we interpret it to be performed. To communicate objective facts as well as subjective feelings by incorporating two categories of conducting. The first, what I call functional conducting, is the communication of specific information. "Here I want a subito-piano." "Here I would like a fermata." "Now I want a release." It is the *what* and *when* of our conducting. It is the science side of conducting. It dispassionately, but precisely, offers specifics of technical performance.

The other type of conducting is what I call impressionistic conducting. This is the portrayal of style, expression, drama, emotion, manner, and feelings. It is the *how* of our conducting. It is the art side of our conducting. It is probably why we became music teachers to begin with! I believe, however, for the impressionistic aspect of our conducting to really work, it must be layered on top of a foundation of functional information. The passion evoked by fits of ecstatic movement are wonderful if they don't forgo clearly conveying the roadmap of technical data needed to correctly execute the composition.

When thinking about the difference between those two types of conducting, I can't help but think of the wonderful story about the conductor who was about to begin a work with his orchestra. In preparation for the downbeat, he began the most theatrical, passionate buildup of motions imaginable. He built to a raging, unbridled, romantic exhibition of twists and turns before suddenly stopping. He looked at his players and angrily said, "You missed the downbeat." To which a player loudly replied, "Oh, we didn't know if you were done! Is it our turn now?" Those players certainly got their fill of the *how*, but with little or no *when*, it was useless.

Obviously, it depends on whether you are conducting the New York Philharmonic or a fourth-grade band, the London Symphony Chorus or a sixth-grade choir. But I believe in my heart of hearts that even the most seasoned of professional ensembles need a little functional conducting. Maybe the New York Philharmonic only needs one percent functional to ninety-nine percent impressionistic and our fourth-grade band needs ninety-nine percent functional to one percent impressionistic, but they both need some of each. Maybe our eighth-grade orchestra will require far more functional than impressionistic conducting as they start rehearsing for the year, but as the weeks pass they will come to *need* far less functional and come to *use* far more impressionistic.

It comes down to asking ourselves whether we are communicating facts as well as feelings. Let me ask you a simple question. You are about to get into your car in Ohio and travel to downtown New York City. This will be your first visit to the Big Apple, so you will need a map. I'm going to give you two choices. Choice one is a map drawn by an impressionistic artist. She will give you that warm and fuzzy feeling of getting-to-New-Yorkishness. Choice two offers you a map drawn by a professional mapmaker. He will use the finest straightedge, most powerful computer, sharpest marker and most accurate tools to detail every aspect of your trip. Which one do you want to use?

That is the question we often pose to our students in rehearsals everyday. Granted, the former can be impassioned, however, it may land you in North Carolina instead of Manhattan. Equally true is the fact that the latter can be boring, antiseptic and mechanical. Sometimes we offer our students a great deal of impressionistic feeling, but they can't figure out what we need them to do functionally. Ernest Hemingway described this dilemma perfectly when he said, "Never mistake motion for action."

Other times, we portray every fact, but with little or no expression. Or said better, to paraphrase the great Erich Leinsdorf, we can't be so concerned with the printed page that we ignore the essence of the music. The best of both worlds would be to have that mapmaker's product enhanced by the addition of the artist's representation of feelings, mood and character. One overlying the other as a composite representation.

Another way of looking at this idea is to think of four words that I use as a mantra of sorts: *context different — content same*. What I mean by the context is the impressionistic aspect of the performance. The style, manner, performance practice and mood of how we execute the technical demands of the work as well as the general character of the work itself. The content, or specific facts, are performance techniques. True, a sforzando or subito-piano in a work from the classical period would be interpreted differently from those found in some compositions written today. However, the fact, or content, is not in question, only the manner with which it is carried out or applied.

In other words, I want my students to recognize my communication of a subito-piano as a fact. Layered on that will be information as to how it should be used.

My fear is that at this point you may be saying to yourself, "This sounds all well and good if you're working with college age students. But what about fifth-graders?" I truly believe this approach works equally well with inexperienced performers. Undoubtedly, the difficulty and expectation level will be different, but the method by which we conduct can be the same. Think of it this way: those fifth-graders have little if any preconceived notion of what conducting is about. We can mold them easily. By the time a student is in high school, it is harder to change his or her impression of what conducting does. By then, they are certain they have seen it all. That clay becomes harder to mold. Harder, but not impossible.

EXPRESSIVE CONTROL

The second goal is to allow you complete control while having the freedom to be expressive. Please don't think for a second I am advocating a lot of little robotic conductors. On the contrary, I hope we can be as expressive and emotive as possible. With effective conducting, we are released from concern over whether an ensemble will understand that we want an accelerando, let alone when and how it is wanted. We will have the mental and physical freedom to be truly expressive. On the other hand, if during a performance that accelerando starts to come unraveled due to a lack of clarity in communication, and all heck starts to ensue, can we or our students be free to emote? If we just hold on for dear life, beat time with flailing motions, and wait it out, we can't be much in the way of expressive. With control over the performance, we are unencumbered. We are free to share with our ensemble in the communicative dialogue of the essence of the music.

Let's pretend you are flying an airplane. Even if your flying skills are only fair, you can certainly hold the yoke steady enough to fly the plane straight and level on a calm day and enjoy the wonders of the view. However, if a sudden gust of wind or turbulence sends the plane into a steep bank, and panic has you start to throw your hands and the controls every which way, or freeze up, it is doubtful you will take note of the beauty outside your aircraft. Through the clarity of control comes the ease of being expressive.

CAUSE AND EFFECT

The third goal is to have our conducting work as *cause and effect*. By this I mean our gestures should be understood well enough to immediately elicit the desired response from our performers. It comes down to me thinking, if I do *this* with my hands, it will cause them to do *that*. I hope my functional communication can be so well understood that it allows performers to *react* instantly to a gesture's meaning, rather than to *act* upon the information, more slowly pondering its meaning.

REACTION TIME

The fourth goal is to take into consideration the *reaction time* needed to allow our gestures to function, rather than *showing gestures as the response is to happen*. If a gesture is not given in a way that allows for the performer to see it, decipher it, react to it, and apply it, that musical outcome will probably occur late. If we show musical events as they happen, our students will have to rely on their memory, rather than the aid of our communications. True, their printed music can assist, but what about our interpretation, or those magnificent musical attributes that defy the written word or symbol?

EXPEDIENT

Rehearsal time is like a clothes closet. No matter how much closet space we have, we want more. As well, the amount of space needed increases as the amount made available increases. If you agree with me that no amount of rehearsal time is ever enough, you will agree that our fifth goal should be that our conducting is expedient. Our gestures should be logical, predicated on the laws of physical motion, thus needing little if any explanation. If the preparation gesture for a down-beat follows the laws of gravity and physics it will be understood.

I ask you to picture an apple tree. See it. Look at those ripe, red apples hanging way up there. One of them is about to fall off the tree. You're going to watch it descend and go splat on the ground. Ready? It's getting riper. Here it goes. Without fanfare, the apple breaks free from its stem and falls to earth. Watch it falling — splat. There it landed. Now let's replay that scene. If you were to close your eyes after the apple started to descend, wouldn't you easily be able to calculate the moment of *the splat* in your mind? This calculation is a result of seeing events like that since you were born and intuitively understanding gravity and physics. It is logical and needs no explanation. If our downbeat is that way, it too will be as simply understood. If, however, that gesture is replete with curlicues and extraneous motions it would need to be interpreted (read: figured out) by our performers. When is the last time you saw an apple fall from a tree with a curlicue motion?

MAKE CONDUCTING A LANGUAGE

Our sixth and final goal is to *use* conducting as a nonverbal language that we can teach to our students. To develop a vocabulary of gestures that give specific information, and to teach and apply them as a foreign language. What the gestures *are* is less important than their being used as a language. Think for a minute. If I were to show you that sign language gesture from earlier in this chapter, would it have any meaning to you? I bet it probably would.

If our conducting is to be used successfully as a language it should follow five basic rules. First, it must be used consistently. If today a gesture means one thing and tomorrow it means something different, it ceases to have meaning. Picture day one of a rehearsal. I teach you that a certain gesture means a subito-piano. Now picture day two of that rehearsal during which I teach you that the same gesture means a forte-piano. When I inquire as to what that object is called on the third day of rehearsal, what do you think I will get as an answer? Can't you just picture one third of the group saying subito-piano, another third saying forte-piano, and a third staring blankly in confusion?

Second, that every motion means something. If we conduct a gesture that is meaningless to our ensemble, either functionally or impressionistically, we don't help the process. In addition, in that human nature often has us ignore what we don't understand, we are teaching them to ignore our communications.

Third, we shouldn't send mixed messages. We are in a rehearsal. We are about to sing a work that begins with extremely soft, elegant and smooth quarter notes. You, my performers, are watching intently. The moment to begin is here. I ready my hands. I offer you the sloppiest, choppiest and most enormous preparation and beat pattern. You start singing just the way I look. I then, in a fit of frustration, yell "no — smoother — softer — more elegant," as I continue to pound out gigantic pulses. That is a mixed message.

Years ago, while studying nonverbal communication, I stumbled upon this as a theory called the double bind syndrome. That syndrome is created when a person offers a message with one language, while simultaneously sending another contradictory message in another language. Though a repulsive thought, if I hit you while I tell you I love you, that is the classic double bind syndrome. While that rehearsal scenario isn't as destructive and reprehensible as the classic example, it is nonetheless illogical and dysfunctional. Mixed messages cause confusion and disconnect or breakdown communications. If, however, all our languages communicate appropriate messages, whether contrasting or complimentary, we can be understood.

Fourth, that we don't *over-conduct*. When I over-conduct, I'm not making the information any more correct, I'm just making it bigger. It's not clearer, there's just more of it. It's like speaking to foreigners. We say something to them. They don't understand. So what do we often do? We shout the exact same words to them, thinking that if it is louder they will understand it better. It doesn't gain meaning with volume, it just gets louder! We need to assess why they don't understand, and find a more appropriate way to communicate. It might only require better enunciation or a different choice of words, but yelling the same meaningless information surely isn't the answer. If a conducting gesture doesn't work, making it bigger or harsher might not be the remedy. We need to assess why it failed, and explore corrections or alternatives. Meaningful gestures don't need to be big, they simply need to be seen.

If our gestures have meaning, and are used consistently, they become a language. Once our conducting functions as a language, it is then easily *transferable*. That ability to be transferred from one situation to the next without alteration, our fifth rule, saves enormous amounts of time. If students learn our gesture for a forte-piano in a work by Mr. Jones, they won't have to unlearn or relearn that gesture to understand a forte-piano in a piece by Ms. Smith. Though the context will be different, the knowledge and application will be transferable.

I hope that each of us can stand in front of our ensembles, and with no explanation, have them understand the meaning of our gestures. Can we get them to start cleanly, irrespective of whether the initial attack is violent or subtle, loud or soft? Can we conduct various rhythms from our imagination and have the ensemble perform those rhythms with us? Can we instruct our performers to sound a tone when we cue them, and randomly cue attacks around the ensemble with control and clarity? Can we conduct a series of different volumes with unmistakable precision? Can we conduct a repeated tone over and over, and clearly communicate a subito-piano somewhere in the passage? Those are lofty goals. But we can achieve them.

We may simply need to approach our conducting from a different viewpoint. Moments when we become displeased with our hands may offer a wonderful opportunity for us to remember the words of Jon Remmerde who wrote, "When one finds himself in a hole of his own making, it is a good time to examine the quality of workmanship." If something doesn't work, that can be the best time to assess why, and to reflect on other possibilities. Rather than allow frustration to prevent us from continuing to grow, we can think of that remarkable Zen saying, "It is better to light a candle than to curse the gathering darkness."

Food For Thought

The balance of this chapter is devoted to describing some very frequent observations about conducting as it is often practiced. We have all seen them on countless occasions. These common mannerisms and gestures are not listed here to be thought of as mistakes. Indeed, many of them are widely used, popular and considered to be a requisite to good conducting. As previously stated, my only purpose is to have us truly think about what we do, not to label anything as an error. They are here for us all to challenge our thoughts on conducting, reaffirming many, and possibly reconsidering some. Do we conduct a certain way because we are blindly following someone else's opinion without ever thinking through the viability and logic of the approach? Do we conduct a certain gesture simply because we have always done it that way, or because we didn't notice we were doing it that way? Have we just become numb to less than desirable aspects of our conducting, like getting used to an odor?

The following observations, some of which you may identify with, are things you may or may not want to do when conducting. It is my hope we can think about each of them, consider whether we do them, and if we do, when and why we use them. As well, we can decide whether we want to be doing them, and if so, do they work, or would something else be more appropriate or useful? We must *each decide for ourselves* whether they are errors or misunderstandings. We are the sole keeper of our convictions, and that is the only way it should be.

STANCE

I believe a conductor's stance can be the source of a great many concerns. The manner with which we compose ourselves, and stand before our ensemble. I ascribe to the belief that our initial stance should offer the performer a blank canvas, a clean slate, a neutral representation void of any communication save that we are serious and ready to go. It should show we are intensely focused on the task at hand, and that we want them to concentrate to the best of their abilities. The power of our capacity to draw them in to us and have them unite as one can almost feel like we are developing tunnel vision around them. The rest of the world begins to evaporate to our sides. The intensity of the bond between us, the open and readied lines of communication increase like suction created by a vacuum. Our collective fervor should be almost palpable. Other than that, we may be working against ourselves.

Would you give Picasso a canvas with a bright fluorescent red dot on it, or a black stripe across it? Probably not. If you did, it would certainly temper what he could say. Likewise, if we have a stance that "says" weak to our ensemble, it becomes difficult for us to express power with our conducting. If we unintentionally communicate violent aggression with our stance it may be impossible to communicate our true desire for a mellow or demure performance. Anything that negatively affects or contradicts our intent may be worth reconsidering. Here are a few examples.

Leaning Forward. Bending forward with the upper torso implies weakness to observers. Just have someone stand in front of you, bent over a bit, as if about to conduct. Can't you just imagine putting words to that picture with a whining voice saying, "Please — oh please — would you kind of think of playing now?" Then have that person stand tall. That undoubtedly will give you more of a feeling of strength and confidence. Though certainly useful for conducting a lament, conducting a majestic and regal passage would be difficult at best while leaning forward in that weakened state.

The Sumo Wrestler. Picture the stance used by sumo wrestlers as they ready to compete. With feet spread extremely far apart, they almost hunch down to gather strength. They look mean and violent. I can almost hear them saying "Come on, give me your best shot!" As a conductor, how can we express angelic calm standing like we are about to wage war?

Jousting. If we stand with one foot in front of the other, like a runner at the ready, we set up an odd canvas for all to see. It forces us to turn our body so that we face to one side. That pulls one arm and hand toward our back, creating an image that one hand is dominant and the other subordinate. How expressive can that subordinate hand be drawn back along your side? The dominant hand always looks like it is held in front of us as if we are about to start jousting with a sword. To correct that situation, many twist their waist, or stretch the retreating arm forward to even out their hands. Either of those adds extra physical strain on muscles, and mental attention to balance and evenness. How comfortable can those remedies be after an hour rehearsal? At the very least we may decide that the jousting stance looks a bit skittish or uneasy. However, the largest problem with that stance is it sets the stage for what I call dissipating energy, which will be discussed later.

Raised Shoulders. If you stand in front of a mirror and raise your shoulders to your ears, you will instantly see a most unusual sight. Then simply drop them to their lowest position and see the image change. It is quite dramatic. Just think what impression you would get from a conductor in that contorted position. Tension, concentration and intensity often get us in that position, which forces us to use extra muscles that can be painful.

Fidgeting. A conductor who fidgets, squirms, twitches or stands with restless movements may have great difficulty gathering that focused attention we spoke of earlier. I ask my students to think how they would stand at the lectern just before addressing the United Nations General Assembly. A sober, still and calm stance will certainly command greater attention and control, and provide you with an opportunity to look in the eyes of every single member of your ensemble. It is a wonderful moment. It only takes a minute, but the benefits are remarkable.

EXTRANEOUS MOTIONS

The following observations include movements or impressions that may be extraneous, work against our desire, or are unintentionally used without benefit. If they are, it is worth reassessing their merit.

Swaying, Rocking and Dancing. As much as we want to start with a blank canvas, we want that canvas to be still. By that I mean our hands and arms move on a backdrop that is our torso. That canvas is the presentation we offer our ensemble. Heaven knows I 'm not saying we should stand still as we conduct. I'm talking about extraneous, unintentional, usually habitual motions that make watching the canvas harder. Swaying is the unintentional moving from side to side as we conduct. Rocking has the upper torso unintentionally moving forward and backward, bending at the waist. Dancing is how I refer to the walking or stepping back and forth, or side to side, as we conduct, like the movement of a pendulum. These movements cause a startling, disconcerting blurred image and distortion of what is seen.

To help with describing what I mean, I 'd like you to think back to elementary school. Do you remember watching movies or slides on a screen that pulled down from the ceiling? If you are like me, you can hearken back to times when that screen was in front of open windows, and every time the wind blew, the screen moved like a giant wave. As it did, the image you were watching got blurry. It was enough to make you seasick, wasn't it?

If our canvas suffers from these unproductive motions, we do the same thing to our students. Sometimes these motions are in time, portraying a pulsating movement, and sometimes they are out of time, offering a wandering motion. Either way, they will usually make it harder for performers to watch, and often lead them to watch less due to the ill-at-ease feeling the motions create.

Curlicues. Have you ever been driving along on a highway and all of a sudden you were traveling around in a giant circle? You know, one of those rotaries. Those spheres of wandering aimlessness. You drive round and round, watching signs go by until you figure out which turn off the rotary is the one you want. Usually the process involves much neck twisting, pointing toward an exit just past (now behind you), and naughty language.

Often, I find curlicues to be the rotaries of conducting. If we find ourselves stranded in the middle of a pattern, unsure where we should go next or how to get there, we sometimes use curlicues to wander around until we figure it out. They are a smooth and elegant way of being a bit lost. If they are used for a purpose they can be magnificent. If they are used as a mask or smokescreen they can be terrifying.

Subdividing. This label is really a misnomer. I don't mean the true conducting of a subdivided beat as in a baroque adagio or an incredibly dramatic rallentando. I refer here to that twitching, bouncing, flitting, hitch-like motion often exhibited like an aftershock of every beat in a pattern. It looks like one's hands are swatting an extra jolt of motion, with the blurring speed of a hornet, on the rebound of every beat. Though it is often used in an effort to provide clarity and precision, it creates clutter and garbled communication of the actual beats. There is so much motion that it is not readable. This is certainly one case where more is less, and less is more.

Multiple Focal Points. Close your eyes. While they're closed, I am going to pose my hands in the air. Each hand will look like a mangled, gnarled tree branch, with odd angles and bent knuckles, fingers stretched out going every which way. My pinky fingers will be aimed outward to the sky, my middle fingers pointed to the floor, my thumbs directed inward to my chest, and my index fingers pointed to my head. In addition, I am holding a baton that is aimed across my chest, and have a puzzled look on my face. If I asked you to open your eyes and stare at me, what would you be looking at? My baton? The goofy look on my face? One of my index fingers or pinkies? There are simply too many things in that pose to distract you or capture your attention.

Years ago, there was an advertisement featuring a photograph of a conductor posed in just such a way. One of my students tore it out of the magazine, circled the photo in highlighter and wrote, "How many focal points can you find?" Where our students would look is a guess, but what is certain is that anything odd or weird draws attention. It's like driving down the highway and seeing an accident in the other lane of traffic. What do we all do? We slow down, turn our heads away from our lane, and look at the accident. We know we shouldn't, but we are drawn to it like a magnet. If you doubt this trait, just try *not* to look at the moustache of someone sporting some foreign object attached to it while you are talking to him. If our conducting hands have some odd feature, like an extended pinky or tensely bent thumb, we can be sure our students will focus on it.

Cupped Hands. I don't think anyone does this intentionally, but whether it is caused by tension, nervousness or lack of confidence in our physical dexterity, it is nonetheless a prime example of something odd or weird distracting our ensemble. This is having either or both hands stiffly forced together, trying to seal every nook, like you are going to use the hand to drink water from a stream. The fingers and thumb are "glued" together while the knuckles jut into an awkward, angled mass of strained anxiety. Not only does it look strange, it causes undue tension and greatly stilted motion in our arms, and stress and anxiety in our players. Looking at that hand position, can our students be anything but tense? To be sure it can't be any more comfortable to watch than it is to do. Simply relaxing the hand will undo all of that tension for both player and conductor.

Wrist Flicking. This is the flapping or slapping of your hands in a downward motion, bending at the wrist like one stroke of waving to someone, on every beat. Unlike the subdivision described earlier, this happens in one fell swoop on each beat, as opposed to the subdivision's echo after the initial beat motion. If you were to see a pattern conducted with wrist flicking, where would you determine the start or point of the beat to be? Is it when the fingers are pointed to the heavens, when they are aimed to the floor, or somewhere in between? The excess motion makes it extremely difficult to read clearly.

Head Bobbing. Think of how much a human head weighs. It's quite heavy (Somewhere in there is a joke, but I don't think I'm the one to make it!). Picture nodding your head up and down on every beat in a bobbing fashion, like one of those toy dogs that used to be seen in the back of some people's cars. The extra energy needed, let alone the wear and tear on the body, is unbelievable. When I see this in a conductor, I get tired and sore just watching. I don't know how anyone can do it for an entire rehearsal. Even more problematic is that the extraneous motion of the head is extremely difficult to decipher, and negates the visual impact of the hands.

CLEAR PREPARATIONS

A highly communicative gesture of preparation for any aspect of a work we wish to convey to an ensemble is our best friend. Whether it is to announce a cue, change an articulation, or signal a cutoff, it is our only true means of non-verbally allowing our students to predict when they are to react. Never is that gesture more obvious than when starting an ensemble, the initial preparation gesture. That split second when we need to take a group of performers from silence to a first attack with precision and control. It can be one of the most debilitating, frustrating and frightening moments. I also believe that poor preparations are the fastest way we develop bad habits. Those bad habits, over time, become so much a part of us as to become entrenched in our approach. As the Spanish proverb states, "Habits are at first cobwebs, then cables."

The Preparation Syndrome. To illustrate how those habits develop, let me take you through what I call *The Preparation Syndrome*. Here is how it starts. We are about to conduct our very first rehearsal. Our supervisor is standing in the back of the room and our ensemble is ready to go. Exuding confidence, we stand in front of our performers and ask them to begin the rehearsal with the playing of a unison concert B flat. Remembering everything we learned in college, we conduct the most perfect preparation. Nothing happens. At that moment, we go into panic mode. Our boss is watching and our students are concerned. Our blood pressure rises. Our heart rate increases. What do we do? So we do it again, but this time we make the preparation gesture gigantic, and whack the heck out of it. We over-conduct, usually making the communication harder to read with lots of extraneous motion. That doesn't improve our result; it's only shouting the same information at a louder volume. This time, we get an attack that sounds like the ensemble is doing "the wave." I think of over-conducting like taking aspirin. One aspirin is possibly fine, two may be perfect, but thirty will probably kill you!

With terror in our hearts, we try a double preparation by adding another beat of motion before the preparation gesture. All that does is confuse the ensemble even more. The result is usually that half of them play after the first motion, thinking you are still only giving one beat of preparation, while the others figure out that you are giving two beats of preparation and wait for the appropriate time. As we start to hyperventilate, we realize what a mess we've created. Next, we add popping our fingers. That's when we make an okay sign with our hands, flicking it open at the moment we want the ensemble to sound. All of that extra motion makes matters worse. They truly can't find the information they need. Where are they to attack? Is it when the okay sign moves? Is it when our index fingers leave our thumbs or is it when our fingers are at their most extended position?

Worrying whether we will have a job let alone a career at the end of this session, we next add a thrusting head motion, or jumping body movement or stamping foot. They don't work, so we finally resort to counting off with, "One — two — ready — play — now!" At that moment, hearing the ensemble play, we are relieved. We escaped. We now believe counting off "worked," and the correct preparation we started with "failed." With that belief, will we ever try the latter again, or will we make counting off a permanent habit? The next time we give a preparation will we be inclined to go through that torture again, or will we immediately go to what we know worked? If what worked is something we don't want to be doing or is counterproductive, we might be stuck with it.

We can't panic. We can stop that chain reaction from happening. We need only to make the gesture clear, easy to read, and truly communicative. Once we know the gesture is sound, we need to hold our ground and try to make it work. After we think the gesture is functional, we can firmly and insistently try it. If we still meet with a lack of success, we need to simply reassess the gesture. We can't panic. Calmly, we need to try another gesture or develop another way of thinking about that gesture. Quite simply, I believe poor preparations lead to bad habits, which lead to bad habits, which lead to bad habits.

The Ruffle. When we give our initial preparation, we often don't get results as awful as what was just described. We often hear the initial attack with what I term "the ruffle." It is a very subtle and devious foe. It is not the obvious playing of many attacks at drastically different times. The ruffle has what appears to be one sound, but it is made up of sixty attacks that are ever so slightly separated in time, but overlap each other. It sounds like the rolling of an R with that "fffrrrahh" coming from the ensemble. It is insidious. It isn't usually wrong enough to make us pause, but it is less than attractive. More importantly, it allows weak communication and sloppy playing to be considered acceptable. Granted, if Steve isn't hitting Sue with the chime mallet, and Henry has the trumpet facing in the right direction, we can often be lulled into accepting the ruffle, but we know they can do better.

Bent Knee Preparation. Picture me standing in front of you. My knees are bent. My torso is leaning back from the waist. My hands and arms are ready to give an initial preparation. All at once, as I conduct my downbeat, I thrust my torso forward while I lock my knees. That bent knee preparation is a very odd, but common occurrence. Though it creates the illusion of a lot of motion, the hands and arms don't move independently of the torso, they move as a result of the torso moving so much. If you picture me leaning back with my hands ready to go, then thrusting forward with my elbows frozen against my body, it looks like my hands have moved a great deal. They haven't. Through all the motion in that gesture, but lack of real hand movement, I have never been able to find the communication.

Looking Down. Though we all know we shouldn't look down to the score at the moment of initial attack, it is so very common. It is such an easy habit to get into. But the lines of communication at that crucial second in time can't be broken. Whether it's staring at the score during our entire preparation, or looking down just as our hands move down, it confounds our ability to communicate. We need their eyes as much as they need ours, especially at those critical times. It is probably the most appropriate application for those immortal words of Bülow, "You must have the score in your head and not your head in the score." We know it; we just can't underestimate its importance.

DISSIPATING ENERGY

In an effort to show power, weight, or accented articulations we often use what feels like a potent and forceful movement that truthfully works against us. Those very movements dissipate all of the energy and strength from our gestures like a lightning-rod on a tall building saps all of the current from a lightning strike into the ground. The following movements, as opposed to maintaining a firm stance which allows no energy to escape, work like a shock absorber soaking up all of the impact of a bump in the road. Here's how they function in our conducting.

Bent Knees. If we bend our knees a great deal as we conduct while trying to firmly pulse with our arms and hands, those flexible knees will absorb most of the energy. They will move like springs to dissipate all of the weight we are trying to communicate.

Jousting. Remember the one-foot-in-front-of-the-other stance we discussed earlier? Usually in that position, a conductor will plant the foot that is farthest back on its toes. That, coupled with the fact that his center of gravity is now shifted forward, leads the foot to bounce with the heel moving up and down. All of the energy he so desperately wants to communicate is lost there. It doesn't make it into his hands; it is removed through that shock absorber foot.

Tapping Foot. If we tap our foot as we conduct, it shifts our weight, forcing us to stand off balance. In addition, that very tapping motion acts to deplete our power by dissipating energy.

Spring Back. If we stand with our waist pushed forward, but our upper back leaning backwards, we set up our ability to siphon all of the energy from our weighted motions. From the side, our body ends up looking like a cent sign with our head as the top vertical line, our back as the curve, and our legs as the lower vertical line in the symbol. With every attack, the curve in our back compresses, removing most of the power that could be going to our arms and hands.

PLACEMENT OF MOTION

Though I am a firm believer in motions being placed where they communicate what we feel the music demands, the following are a few observations we may want to reconsider if we feel they are hindering our communication.

Conducting High. If we think about the laws of motion, nature and gravity we probably can agree that height usually implies lightness or weakness. Watch yourself in a mirror as you conduct with your pattern up above your head. Now conduct the same pattern just above your waist. Does one offer you the feeling of weight and the other weakness? If you believe it does, you can use those impressions to help make your communication more congruent with the music. When conducting high, I think it is as difficult to show power and weight as it is easy to show lightness and finesse.

Three-Dimensional Conducting. If we watch a conductor from the back center of an ensemble, I believe we come to realize conducting is far more two-dimensional than three-dimensional. A large motion, moving directly forward, has less impact from that vantage-point than a small gesture moving vertically or horizontally. Granted, anyone on the sides can see it well, but with my previously stated worries about the dead zone, that doesn't help. I think motions from front to back and back to front can be exciting, dramatic and vibrant. I only mention them here so we think about how visible they actually are and what impact they truly make.

Conducting Ourselves. Whenever I see conductors doing this, I always think to myself that they must be having the best time. They look so happy and fulfilled. This is when our elbows are stretched out in front of us, our fingers aimed toward each other with our palms pointing to our face. Conducting this way looks as though we are aiming all the communication to *us*. In the back of our head it's like we are saying to ourselves, "...oh baby — you look good — look at that left hand...." It looks great from *our* eyes, but our ensemble sees mostly elbows and knuckles. There is an enormous amount of motion with very little communication. That motion is often distorted and negates the power of the hands almost entirely.

INDEPENDENCE OF HANDS

One of the most important things a conductor can bring to the podium is the ability to use true independence of hands. Without question, there are times we may want to have our hands mirroring each other. At other times we may want one arm at our side, conducting with only one hand. But sometimes using one hand to express one communication, while the other hand offers another, is helpful to the ensemble and evocative of the music. If the brass sustain a line, while the woodwinds break the phrase dramatically, wouldn't it be wonderful to show both aspects of the music simultaneously?

If we develop that ability to the point where we have complete confidence, we will be free to communicate, possibly like never before, providing yet another dimension of our ability to emulate sound in motion. Even if we don't wish to go to that extent, working on our independence of hands will enhance those movements that require some of that ability, like turning pages and offering cues. But whether it is showing two different rhythms, dynamic levels, phrases, articulations, or moods, that skill can be extraordinarily communicative. Rather than instruct the ensemble about two simultaneously occurring contrasting articulations, we can show both. If one needs to be exaggerated more, we can communicate that with our hands instead of our mouth.

PATTERNS

There are as many opinions about patterns as there are books and approaches to conducting. We could discuss this topic for years and not scratch the tip of the iceberg. I only mention it here to offer three observations that we can think about as we apply our art.

Logical. Do our patterns follow the laws of science, especially those of gravity, and are they logical to figure out? For example, if our patterns have motions that more resemble roller coasters than bouncing balls, we may have a problem with the logic of the pattern. When I think about a pattern with lots of curlicues and overlapping loops, I ask myself if I have ever seen an apple fall from a tree that makes that motion, or a wave in the ocean move that way.

Flow. Certainly, one thing common to every approach to conducting I have ever seen is that we need to have the ability to show flow. That continuous motion from one pulse to the next, one measure to the next, or one phrase to the next. Can we portray continuous motion rather than communicate choked-off, stagnant pulsations? Though we need to have the ability to emulate both, the former usually gives more of us reason to pause. That fluid motion, pulling of taffy, or stretching of sound we desire can be a challenging goal.

Beating Time. Though I am the first one to say there are times when the best thing we can do for our performers and the music is simply to beat time, it can *become* the norm. If the line is homorhythmic, could we conduct that rhythm rather than beat time? Do we need to beat time during rests?

When I present this chapter as a conference session I always ask the audience to sing a certain pitch with whatever rhythm I conduct. Without music, they sing a "composition" consisting of various rhythmic durations I communicate to them with my conducting. Other than the host for the session reading my mind and telepathically writing those rhythm patterns on the board behind me, there can only be one explanation for this to work. The gestures must communicate the functional information about those rhythms, and do so in a fashion that allows enough reaction time that the performers can act upon them in tempo. Gestures such as those not only communicate valuable information, they more accurately reflect the music itself.

DYNAMICS

I think the key to successfully communicating dynamics is proportional and consistent information. Whatever way we choose to show dynamic levels, those gestures need to be used consistently so as to maintain their function as a language. If today this size pattern means forte, and tomorrow that size pattern means triple forte, our ability to communicate diminishes. In addition, those gestures need to be proportional in size to each other as well as to our body size. That creates a framework of gestures for dynamics that is logical. We also need to have the ability to communicate sudden dynamic contrasts such as subito-piano, subito-forte and forte-piano, so that those musical events are communicated with gestures representing precise meaning rather than the often seen flurry of movement that lacks clarity.

CUEING

Many feel that too much cueing leads to performers becoming reliant on the conductor. That may be true, but I think the opposite is even more fraught with danger. I remember once attending a party at a friend's home. One of the world's great orchestral musicians was there. Over coffee I asked, "Do you ever feel that cues from the conductor are sophomoric, or an insult?" Without missing a beat he said, "No. It is always nice to know you're right."

I hope to offer as many cues as I can without negatively impacting the essence of the music. If I can help a performer to know he or she is right, I will. So often cues seem to fail to get us the desired result. I think that is due to our cueing either too late (at the moment it is to sound, thus not allowing for reaction time), or without sufficient use of our eyes. Don't you think eye contact is more often than not how performers read a cue, with the hands just coming along for the ride? I really don't mean to diminish the power of the hands to cue, but I do hope to heighten our awareness of how powerful the eyes can be to that end.

TEMPO

Few things in this world can cause conductors to have fear well up in their being like the feeling of having a piece start to "pull away" from their indicated tempo. It's like the feeling of a car driving away while you are still trying to get into it. Establishing a tempo rarely gives us a problem; it's keeping that tempo that can be maddening. The following motions are most often used in an effort to retrieve or hold our tempo once we sense that loss of control.

Overreacting. One of the most difficult techniques for a pilot to learn is to fly a course from one point directly to another in a straight line. It seems as though it should be easy, doesn't it? It isn't. What usually happens is that we start off beautifully, then realize that we are moving slightly off course to the left. At that moment, we correct for the error by turning to the right. Unfortunately, we overcorrect, and end up going too far in that direction. So what do we do? We turn to the left, but again go too far and overcorrect. The result of all this is that we fly what looks like a serpentine of movements to the left and right in an effort to fly straight.

That is exactly what so often happens as we conduct. We want a steady tempo. When they start to slow, we speed up. However, we end up going a bit faster just to make sure they catch up to us. They unfortunately get to our tempo, but often continue to go even faster. So what do we do? We slow down. Then they slow down even more, and on it goes. Our tempo resembles the swinging of a pendulum, hitting the center point only to continue to move on before swinging just as exaggeratedly in the opposite direction. Pilots learn that very small corrections that are held firmly yield a much better result than gross overcorrecting that chases after the goal. We can set a tempo, stick with it, and make them come to us.

Too Much Information. In an effort to maintain a very fast tempo with precision, we often conduct a pattern of beats that goes by so fast as to look like the wings of a hummingbird. If we conduct pulses moving at two hundred forty beats per minute, we may look more like we are trying to takeoff than portray music. Would the composition be better served if we conducted it in a hypermeter? Would the clear communication of cut-time pulses be easier to read than common time pulsations of extremely rapid speed? Would conducting every beat of a triple meter moving like lightning be better read than the clarity of conducting that with one beat to the measure? The answer may not be obvious, but experimenting, when results are not what we would like them to be, may be helpful.

Too Little Information. If we conduct pulses that are too slow we may lose the ability to control the ensemble. Like a sailboat in the water, with no forward speed, it is impossible to control the boat with the rudder. We need enough momentum to allow us to keep control.

Popping Fingers. So often when our tempo starts to unravel, we add the popping of fingers, described earlier for preparations, to the mix. Some people are convinced this gesture adds specificity to the point of each beat, hence clarifying the tempo. In that the gesture lacks specificity, and adds incredible amounts of extraneous information, I believe it makes matters worse. In situations like that, *less* information that is clear, beats (no pun intended) more information that clutters the view.

Tilting Torso. When our concern for tempo slipping really becomes desperate, we often resort to the tilting torso. That is when our entire upper torso, bending at the waist, moves forward and backward as if our head was a bass drum beater hitting an imaginary instrument. It is clearly an effort to make our intentions firm. Sadly, there is so much movement, it is virtually impossible to find the tempo. In addition, since *so much of us* is in motion, the motions often are at a slower rate than we really want.

CONDUCTOR OR DIRECTOR

Much of what we have been addressing boils down to the question of *who* we want to be when we are on the podium. I believe that there are two of us in that body of ours standing on the box. Both are integral and essential parts of being a wonderful and effective educator.

The first person I call the *director,* irrespective of whether it is band director, choir director or orchestra director. You are a verbal being, "explaining" most of what is communicated, transmitting information from your voice to the performers' ears. That makes your efforts very time-consuming, and only useful in rehearsals. In addition, that very characteristic serves to lessen the importance of your hands as a way of communicating. It also reinforces a notion that watching the conductor is less important, in that all the direction needed will be heard rather than seen.

The second person is the *conductor.* You are a nonverbal being, communicating everything from your body to the performers' eyes. In that you are nonverbal, you communicate in silence, which is equally effective in rehearsal and concert. You don't need to give lengthy explanations, so you communicate almost instantly. With every motion or gesture, with every successful communication, you reinforce the necessity and virtues of watching.

I don't think the question is *which* of those we want to be. Both are necessary, vital and indispensable. The question is *what proportion* of each do we want to be? Have we developed both parts of our director/conductor personality? Are we comfortable and effective with either of them? The ability to adjust the amount of each used at any given time is what makes us teachers. We sense when students need and should have explanation, but require them to move on to the open vista that is nonverbal communication.

NOW THAT WE'VE THOUGHT

I have a love-hate relationship with video cameras and mirrors. Do you know what I mean? The more time I spend watching myself conduct in the mirror or viewing videotapes of rehearsals, the more I value their usefulness, but hate their lack of forgiveness. They are, however, the best way for us to truly assess what we *are* doing on the podium, as opposed to what we *want* to be doing. If something doesn't work, we will know it. Then we can, as Willie Jolley says, "face it, trace it, erase it, and replace it." We can come to terms with the fact that it isn't getting the desired result. Trace the reason why. Erase the gesture from use in that situation. Then we can move on to the most enjoyable part, replacing it with something else. Here we get to use every ounce of creativity we have.

After we come up with a replacement, all we can do is try it. If it works, great. If it doesn't, we try again. As Eloise Ristad said, "...it is such a luxury to know that it is not only permissible to fail part of the time, but an essential ingredient of being human. And we find that the failing is not failing after all, but merely learning." That remarkable advice is just what we would tell our students, so what's good for the goose...! We just need to be creative; better still, we need to enjoy *being* creative, in the process of assessing our conducting as well as enhancing our conducting. In the words of Mark Twain, "You can't depend on your eyes when your imagination is out of focus." As said succinctly by Norman Vincent Peale, "See the possibilities."

Our conducting can be a tool to help us gain the precision and communication necessary to have students reach for the stars, and touch them. To bring a composition to life. To portray the depth of emotion in music and our collective humanity. Our conducting must free us from worry about the mundane, so we may savor the beauty of our art and the wonder of our students. The less doubt we have about our ability to communicate with our hands, the more we can emote and be a mirror for our students to see the joy of music.

As you think about what has been discussed in this chapter, I ask that you simply reflect upon it, and use it as that source of food for thought. If you agree with anything, that is wonderful. If you disagree, that's just as good. What does matter is that we continue to challenge our beliefs and develop our skills to help our students reach their goals. As Socrates said, "I believe that we cannot live better than in seeking to become still better than we are."

"PUT YOURSELF IN A STRAIGHTJACKET AND DANCE A FREE DANCE."

You must be asking yourself what that title could possibly have to do with the teaching of music. Let me attempt an explanation. Years ago, I had the incredible pleasure of writing composer Vaclav Nelhybel's biography. We worked for several years together on that project. The preceding quote comes from a story Nelhybel told me about an event that took place just after World War II. Nelhybel wrote his doctoral dissertation on the renowned composer Igor Stravinsky. In describing his dissertation, Nelhybel recalled many wonderful stories. My favorite was his recollection of going to see the world premiere of *The Rake's Progress* in Italy with Stravinsky himself. After the performance, they sat at an outdoor café and talked. Stravinsky told Nelhybel that the goal of a composer was to "Put yourself in a straightjacket and dance a free dance." As Vaclav said those words, I was filled with a remarkable sense of awe. Obviously, Stravinsky meant that the parameters and limitations of a certain commission, or the self-imposed confines of form, style or technique of the process forced the composer to put himself in the constraint of being in a straightjacket. While in that state, though, the composer would need to shape something that was free, creative and seemingly boundless.

Those profound words have stuck with me ever since. Years later, still absolutely infatuated with this quote, I was stopped at an interminably long traffic light on our campus and it hit me. It hit me like a ton of bricks. I realized that as perfect as those words were to describe the art of composition, they are even more perfect to describe the art of conducting. I was exhilarated, elated and invigorated at the thought of how this wonderful statement was the perfect advice for any conductor. I realized that indeed this credo applies to a composer; however, much of that constraint is self-imposed, changeable and based upon creative concerns, but for the conductor the straightjacket is made of constraints almost entirely beyond his or her control. The composer hands a work to the conductor. The rules, instructions, and data are right there. We are told to do what is on the page. Take the dots and markings of the composer's pen and make them into sounds that accurately represent his or her wishes. This can be very daunting, challenging and also seemingly limiting. It isn't, it's joyous!

Once we realize the sheer enjoyment of studying a score, we will become addicted to doing it. We will cherish and savor the process whereby we will come to understand the composer's desires. We'll go beyond simply reading the score. We can put that straightjacket on, and then find artistic and creative wiggle room while we realize and interpret the composer's wishes. We can dance a free or inventive dance while staying bound by the instructions and intent of the composer. As Harold Schonberg stated, "Any interpretive act is a process of refraction, the interpreter being a prism through which the composer's thought is refracted." What artistic joy that can be! Be creative.

At this point I must state that I firmly believe a conductor must follow the letter of the composer's score. I feel it is our duty and obligation. I am crazed at the thought of a conductor changing a work. That is not our job or our privilege. As Hans Swarowsky, a disciple of Richard Strauss stated, "This is your Bible or your Koran or whatever it is where you come from. You will adhere to this completely. In here you will find everything there is to know...When you make a *rubato*, when you take a liberty of any kind, you had better find something in here that told you to do that. Because if you do something that is not written in this book, then you have broken all Ten Commandments at once." We need to develop a keen artistic conscience. Always mindful of the words of Japanese mime Masumi Kuni: "Creativity without discipline is ugly. Discipline without creativity is brutal, but disciplined creativity is beautiful." Or as Toscanini put it, "The oddest thing about conductors, even the best of them, is the way they hold a score up to the light or turn it back to the front. They are always looking for something that isn't there and never see what is."

With that said, I do think there are many times when a composer's exact indications can be used, but more than just the obvious can be extracted. We can go beyond that. Great artistic fancy can be created within the specifics of the composition. For example: exaggerating phrase indications to foster a less obvious structure than that which may be assumed, taking advantage of nebulous indications or non-specific language to allow freedom of creativity, using tone colors to enliven a work, and the releases of phrases to provide differing impressions through overlap or space. These are only a handful of ideas. The point: as you study a work look for opportunities to go on a road less traveled.

Renowned English horn soloist Thomas Stacy put it so perfectly when he said, "The important thing is to open secret doors for your listeners." He went on to say, "No one can do the impossible, but it's fun to do the unlikely." Billy Joel, in *The Performing Songwriter* said, "I have a theory that the only original things we ever do are mistakes." So take a chance to find new ideas or interpretations even if it means making mistakes! I certainly am not saying to ignore the obvious or to abandon tradition. But remember what Toscanini said, "Tradition is laziness." Again, I think of those remarkable words by Paul Creston referenced in the previous chapter: "One must distinguish that which is traditional because it is right from that which is right only because it is traditional." Albert von Szent-Györgyi said it best: "Discovery consists of seeing what everybody has seen and thinking what nobody has thought."

Try coming up with interesting, novel or intriguing concepts of performance that follow the letter of the composer's wishes but are less obvious or conspicuous. To me this is the most enjoyable, creative and exciting aspect of score study. It allows you to make your mark on a work. To make it better than itself. To view it and allow others to view it through your eyes. The choice is whether you want to put on that straightjacket of the score and sit in the corner of the room lamenting the confines of the bondage, or embrace the challenge of dancing a free dance within those constraints. It should make one tingle at the prospect of that possibility. Seize the opportunity. As renowned artist Paul Gauguin said, "I shut my eyes in order to see."

How many of us get that excited about studying a score? Is it simply a necessary evil? Why don't we enjoy studying a score? Do we always have a score at arm's reach so we can grab a few minutes here and there to study? Do our friends accuse us of always having our heads buried in a score? I remember watching a television sitcom about a person who collected those now-famous beanie babies. During the episode a family member, concerned about the frighteningly apparent addiction, confronted the person in his home. While walking around the house, they opened a closet from which hundreds of the little stuffed animals fell. Then they opened kitchen cupboards, the oven, the refrigerator, the freezer, and the bathroom vanity, all from which beanie babies fell like rain. It then dawned on me: why aren't we teachers the same way with scores? Why aren't scores hiding everywhere in our homes and offices for moments of study throughout our days like a dieter stashing chocolate bars around the home? Why don't we all view the joys of score study as solace from our hectic and sometimes less than artistic days? Why don't we all love to study scores? I think it is that many of us have not found the joy of studying a good score.

Over the years, I continually have been asked two specific questions about score study: *why* I love to study scores, and *how* I study a score. Let me try to answer the more important one, the why. I love to study scores to discover the artistic beauty of what has been created by the composer, and then interpret that work with my vision. But most importantly, I love to study scores to be as prepared as I possibly can to teach.

Of all the characteristics of a wonderful conductor and teacher, being prepared must number among the most important. If a conductor is unprepared, he will be relatively useless and ineffective. It is a most frustrating, discouraging, amusical, and unenjoyable experience. At first going into a rehearsal unprepared is often overlooked by a conductor as a one-time event, in that time did not allow for preparation for *that* rehearsal. He basically gets through the rehearsal. Then that starts to happen more and more frequently. Over time, the feeling of being unprepared slowly gives way to a false sense of security. The person ends up subconsciously deciding that he can learn the score on the podium in that he can learn the music faster than the ensemble, and thus stay "one step ahead." Now what were originally thoughts lamenting the notion of going to a rehearsal unprepared, change to thoughts negating the necessity for preparation. That is a formula for concern. We can certainly come up with rationalizations for not preparing our scores, but I truly believe any work, of any difficulty level, if worthy of being rehearsed and performed, is worthy of being studied and prepared. True, a simple grade one piece undoubtedly will take far less time and be far more straightforward to learn than a grade six composition. But they both need to be learned. We all know that *easy* is not a license to "wing it" on the podium. But truthfully I think that cycle of not studying scores stems from discomfort and frustration, or having not found enjoyment, from past study.

The conductor who has truly prepared a work will allow his or her ensemble to progress at a far greater speed with better results and thus more accurately represent the composer's wishes. With a piece learned, the conductor is always steps ahead of an ensemble, prodding forward with anticipation. The unprepared conductor, however, reminds me of the old joke about the pilot who announced to the passengers that he had good news and bad news. The good news was that they were traveling at record speed, with perfectly clear skies, at optimum altitude and with a strong tail wind. The bad news was that they were *lost*. No matter how good a musician the conductor may be, he or she will be rehearsing with little idea to what end.

Let's picture an unprepared conductor rehearsing a section of a work of some complexity. He has the group play through the spot. He then has them play the spot again. While having them play it yet again he assesses the difficulty or problem, tries to figure out what is going on, how to fix it, and how to conduct it in a way to help the players. That takes time. Sadly, I have found that type of conductor more often simply has the ensemble repeat the passage several times with hopes of the problem fixing itself. Then he moves on, usually with the mistake or problem in tow. Either way that consumes the most precious commodity we have: time.

Let us now envision the same scene with a conductor who knows the score cold. More than likely, that error would never have occurred. The prepared conductor would have studied that spot and determined the best way to conduct it to cause the players to execute it correctly, or would know what to tell the players to look out for to avoid the problem. If there was a problem, the prepared conductor would have already known where the problem was, what was wrong, and what was needed to do to fix it. That is efficiency. That saves time. Picture a forty-five minute rehearsal done by each of those two conductors. Now envision the progress each ensemble would have made. I always ask myself in which group I would want to be playing. Whenever we watch the rehearsal of a conductor who really knows the score, we look on in awe as he or she rapidly moves from measure to measure correcting problems, offering abundant cues and executing gestures with surgical precision.

We all appreciate this ability when we see it. Then why don't we all prepare better? Often I think we either feel we don't have the time or the tools to prepare scores to the best of our ability. As for the time, without question the energy requirements of our jobs, with all the challenges, duties and responsibilities of a conductor and teacher, make for a harried and draining day. The paperwork, phone calls, and administrative duties can all but sap a person's time, let alone energy. The result, more often than not, is that the first thing to go is the most vital aspect of our job.

What gets the short end of the stick is you, the artist. That is the problem. I think what we need to do is allow the short time we have each day to *make music* be as exciting, fulfilling and vibrant as possible. We must allow that brief time to be a musical and artistic oasis. A time when you can concentrate on nothing but helping people make music. The reason you became a teacher and conductor in the first place was to savor the moments of musical joy and beauty. To that end, for us to accomplish all we can, and more importantly to help our students accomplish all they can, we need to be as prepared as possible. We must find the time to make ourselves feel happy, artistically fulfilled and pedagogically ready. It must be our first priority. We owe it to ourselves. We owe it to our students. We owe it to our art. We must take care of and nourish our artistic souls. We can all come up with many rationalizations why being prepared can't work with our ensembles: ability of the players, a flawed schedule, the administration, the shape of the room, the feeder system, or the cycle of the moon being out of phase with the sun on the third Thursday of a month with the letter R in it. But are all of those just cover for the fact that we don't feel comfortable with our approach to learning and studying scores?

Studying scores — some people tremble at the very thought. I think for some that notion conjures up feelings of drudgery. For many, score study was described in a way that made it sound less than fun. The question I hear is often expressed as simply as, "How do you start?" Many people describe to me the same feeling I often have when I start writing a new article. I sit there ready to go, staring at a blank computer screen with no idea how to start. At those times, the most salient thought pulsing through my brain is, "ah...ah?" I believe many conductors end up settling for being unprepared because they become frustrated every time they try to study a score. Finding no relief from this frustration, the inevitable becomes reality. As with any skill, I am sure if you feel confident with your score study abilities, you are wondering why this chapter exists. You are thinking, "What do you mean *how* do you study a score, you just do it." I remember attending a clinic by a renowned flute soloist, who after playing with the most beautiful vibrato was asked by a member of the audience how to execute that magical sound. The answer was simply, "You just do it," which was followed by another playing of the same passage. To those who can study a score it is like walking; you just do it. To someone who is thin, the answer to being overweight is easy: you just lose weight. To someone who never smoked, the answer to cigarette addiction is equally simple: you just stop smoking. However, to those who are frustrated by the task, or who don't know where or how to start, the following is a simple guide to start you off. It provides aspects of inductive as well as deductive reasoning, and will allow for an individual's own pace. Though great authorities on the subject have detailed the enormous and fascinating pursuit of these challenges in books, articles, lectures and papers, what follows is simply here as a way to get started on the road to score study enjoyment. In no way should this be thought of as exhaustive or complete, but like the famed twelve-step approach to dealing with addictions, the following will offer a starting place for you to accomplish your goals that will fit in with the time demands of your job.

When discussing score study, two questions always arise: the use of solfege or piano, and the use of recordings to learn a score. I use a combination of a great deal of solfege and a small amount of piano playing. Why? I am comfortable with, confident using, and enjoy solfege, and I am a pretty bad piano player. I have had students who study scores much more by piano than voice because they are pianists. That is great! However, my piano playing aside, I truly believe that the use of solfege is a far better way of really learning a work. It forces the audiation of parts and the realization of the work in one's mind. I have seen many a fine pianist play a score and take with him little in the way of understanding. Each conductor must do what is appropriate for him or her, but don't take the easiest way out; it may not be the best. My recommendation is for singing with solfege whenever possible, reserving the piano for complex harmonic passages and connective tissue. The ratio of these will vary from person to person and composition to composition.

As to the use of recordings to "learn" a score, I am a firm believer that this is the worst way to learn (if you can call it that) a score. I'm not talking about using reference recordings to find new works of interest, but rather learning a work by listening to a recording over and over. Some believe that by listening to it they will come to know it well. I believe all they will come to know is how someone else correctly or incorrectly interpreted the work. Even listening to the best of recordings negates the joy of studying a work. You end up copying the work, not learning it. This is a time to reinvent the wheel. You need to start from scratch and learn every note so as to come up with your very own interpretation of the work.

My favorite story about this goes back to my undergraduate school days and one specific conducting class. The final exam for that class was to conduct a movement from a very complicated work. The teacher admonished us that we were not to listen to recordings, but to learn the work ourselves. A few students failed the exam. When they inquired about their grades, the teacher responded by stating that the grade was a result of the fact that they had listened to a recording of the work. In amazement, the students, who *had* listened to a record in the library, could not figure out how he knew. We later found out he had removed every recording of the work from the library, except for one. That one had several glaring tempo and meter errors in the performance. The teacher could easily recognize those errors replicated by the students. I was delighted I hadn't taken that path, and learned a valuable lesson in the process. As Henri Matisse put it, "There is nothing more difficult for a truly creative painter than to paint a rose, because before he can do so he has first to forget all the roses that were ever painted."

Think of where we would be in medical research if all any scientist did was to copy the same experiment of a more learned colleague. We would at best never invent anything new, and at worst simply perpetuate previous mistakes. In addition, remember that we are dealing with an art and science. There are often no rights and wrongs. You may not find anything new in your study. However, you may find a unique way of interpreting something that is not necessarily better than others, but is your own. Don't give away that right by simply copying a record. Think of it this way: if you were to move into a new home, would you want to keep the previous owner's furnishings or bring your own? Keep the parameters of the home, but make it your own interpretation.

To prove my point about this in my conducting classes, I give every student a sheet of paper with three lines drawn on it. As I hand it to them, I tell them to hold the page just as I gave it to them. I then tell them to study that drawing of a chicken foot. I go on and on about the nuances of that chicken foot. I then ask them what they are holding a drawing of. They firmly reply, "a chicken foot." I then ask them to study it again, this time from any angle and see if they can envision something else. After time, they release their previous learning and see on the page a drawing of the backside of a woman. I can then share with them that they were actually looking at a drawing by Picasso, entitled *Femme*. By simply regurgitating what they were told, they just repeated *my* incorrect interpretation. As Tom Wilson in his cartoon strip had Ziggy say, "Sometimes you need to lose your reasoning in order to find your reason!!"

With all that said, I do believe recordings have a great place in the study process. *After* we have truly studied the score, developed our own interpretation, had many rehearsals to re-evaluate our study, and some time to cogitate about the work, then listening to many recordings of the work becomes beneficial. Make certain, however, that the timing of when those listenings occur will allow ample rehearsal time to make interpretive changes and teach those changes to the ensemble. After listening to other people's interpretations don't immediately yield your opinion to theirs. Assess what they have done and compare it to your vision of the work. You may find you like your interpretation best. You may also find interpretations of others you may decide to try, ideas to experiment with in future rehearsals, or mistakes in your interpretation you will need to correct.

I also would try to listen to a definitive recording of the work at this point. By that I mean one: conducted by the composer, overseen by the composer, conducted by the commissioning conductor who studied the work with the composer, or conducted by a student of the composer or an authority on that composer. Though that can be invaluable, do not rely on them either to learn the work. Use them as a reference. Be ever vigilant in your ideas of who is an authority, and bowing your opinion to theirs. Our profession is riddled with stories of composers hearing a work conducted by a renowned person that was performed wonderfully, but not even recognizable as their own. I have often heard composers quite frankly say *not* to listen to a certain recording because it is absolutely wrong. My final thought on the subject is this: I figure that I make more than enough of my own mistakes in life without also repeating those of other people. Anyone can copy; an artist is needed to interpret. Be an artist.

What is interpretation? What should all of this score study yield? What is the goal? Is it to find *the answer*? The right or wrong? The cure or solution? No. It is simply to arrive at a *learned opinion*. That is interpretation. All too many conductors are so afraid of being wrong that they never take the chances necessary to be right. By right, I mean to develop their own, learned, reasoned, researched opinion. I truly believe it is great to be correct, it is perfectly wonderful to go out on a limb and be wrong, but it is an awful waste of talent, energy and passion to be wishy-washy, ambivalent or unwilling to learn enough to develop an opinion. That always reminds me of the line about the stock market: you can be a bull, or a bear, but you can't be a pig. You may come up with ideas that some would call incorrect, or some that would be called wonderful, but if you never come to any learned opinion you are doomed never to feel the joys of creativity provided by the study of a composition.

I am not in any way advocating that we need to be know-it-alls or egomaniacs. I am saying that we need to study, research and think enough to come up with an opinion that we can defend and use as a goal for all subsequent rehearsal efforts. However, all the while we should allow for a change of opinion based on continuing study, new sources of information, revised editions, or the great possibility of being wrong. That is what makes for a learned opinion as opposed to a know-it-all possessing "the" answers.

That learned opinion comes from sincere, time-consuming score study and research. It cannot come from learning a score on the podium during rehearsals or from an attitude of score study as being painful. It should be viewed as a joyous time of putting all of one's abilities to the challenge of artistic endeavor, not a necessary evil. I can't picture Einstein waking up one morning with thoughts of, "I have to come up with that *darn* theory of relativity. Well, I guess I better get it over with!"

To conclude these evangelical ramblings let me say that I firmly, passionately believe that some people are afraid to take the first step. Fear, intimidation, personal insecurities and feelings of confronting an enormous task have frozen many. Trust me that if we simply start to study a score in the following ways, with no pressure or preconceived worries, we will gradually become addicted. Taking the first step of a long journey is always the hardest. Not because it is any harder, but because of all the mental anguish that comes with it. A single step in a journey is a step, whether it is the first or last. Take the first step with the same enthusiasm and confidence that you would take the last one. If score study sounds like the taste equivalent of sucking on a lemon, I believe now is the time to start making lemonade.

Before moving on, we need to discuss two very controversial topics regarding score study: memorization and the marking of the score. Advocates of different sides of these issues tend to be firm in their beliefs. I sometimes think it would be easier to discuss religion than these two topics. My thoughts are neither novel nor adamant. I believe we should know a score by memory well enough to conduct it with certainty. We should have studied the composition enough that this is not a difficult task. I also believe we should have marked the score, in the study process, in a way that would foster the recall of less obvious, buried, or subtle details. Then, coupling those two ideas, glancing at the score while conducting, I believe we have the best of both worlds. As Stokowski said, "In my opinion the ideal way is to conduct with the score, and yet know the music from memory."

I truly believe that when either of those two topics are taken or preached to extreme opinion it is really an effort to force the necessary score study on those who are less than motivated. By that I mean if I require a score to be conducted by memory, it requires the conductor to "learn" the score. If I were to require the exhaustive use of multiple color pencils and various shapes to re-mark every dot on the score, I really just am trying again to insure that a conductor truly studies every dot.

Some may need to learn a score by marking it with abandon, while others may need to force themselves to conduct by memory to insure the learning is complete. Both can be tools to accomplish the goal of studying and knowing a composition. If either or both facilitate your learning the score better, then by all means incorporate them into your routine. My fear is that either should not be viewed as a panacea or shorthand method of score study. Memorization of surface level information, enough to surely conduct a work by memory, is not learning a score. Marking every ink drop on the page with a highlighter does not mean the work has been assimilated or absorbed.

By way of example, if I ask you to "learn" the route to the airport from my house by memorizing a list of directions, you will learn the required course, and be able to get there. However, will you understand the whole map? Will you come to know the relationship of other roads to the road you are on? Will you note and learn about the sites of interest along the way? Will you come to understand the characteristics and interrelationships of areas and regions of the city you are traveling through? Will you learn why the various streets are named as they are? Will you understand about the architecture of the buildings along your route, or anything other than blindly following the directions: turn right here, go three blocks, turn left...? Likewise, if I ask you to highlight all the lines of a certain chapter of a book, you can do so without even reading them, let alone truly understanding them or their relationship to other lines. To reiterate, both of these techniques are wonderful devices to help in the process of learning a score. They are not cures in and of themselves or even barometers of how well that task has been accomplished.

Generally, I find most conductors who work from memory conduct in broad strokes, in generalities. The impression and overall flow is wonderful. However, I find a lot of the small details of the work are not conducted. Obviously, this is a generalization, but nonetheless an observation. In addition, I find they conduct much of the same music on a regular basis and are less inclined to conduct a great number of different works. I almost get the feeling that they memorize several works then continually conduct them. Though that is not necessarily bad, it is contrary to my wish to conduct as much different music as I can. My motto is taken from a dear friend who has often said, "So much music, so little time."

The wonderful aspect of conducting by memory is that it fosters eye contact and direct communication with an ensemble as well as not having the encumbrance of turning pages. The trick is to know the score so well that it does not become a problem or inhibitor, but rather a catalyst of ideas you would have forgotten. We all know that we should never be reading a score when we conduct, but rather glancing at it to recall previously studied information. It is my impression we generally remember eighty-five percent of the work when we conduct by memory. If we know the score that well, and then use it, we start with eighty-five percent and have the potential for most all of the rest. However, the score must be known well enough so that it does not get in the way of our conducting, our eye contact with the players, or our artistic freedom. If that is the case, we will indeed have the best of both possibilities.

Do not use this reasoning for not-conducting-by-memory as a justification or rationalization for not studying a work well enough to have it memorized. On a regular basis we should close the score or walk out in front of the podium and conduct the work from memory. This will help us check to see if we are as prepared as we should be. When I see some of the greatest conductors in history work with score, I realize this is a logical compromise that facilitates optimum results. Obviously, the level of complexity of a work will dictate the decision much of the time. For example, I can't think of a reason to *not* memorize a very simple work with few minute details. With a more complicated work, no matter how much you know by memory, with the score, you will know even more.

With regard to score markings, my basic admonition is that fewer is better. Fewer colors, fewer markings and fewer words are most useful. I believe the more we mark, the less impact it has on us. Think of a blank white canvas. One drop of red ink will have enormous impact, while thousands of red dots become almost meaningless. How do we see the forest for the trees? There are so many colors and so many marks, we can't see the notes themselves. Remember at all times we are not reading the score or reading our markings. We should glance down occasionally to be reminded of what was already learned and studied. A score is like a prompter on an opera stage. When a singer forgets a line the prompter says one word, just enough to refresh the singer's memory. The prompter does not read the entire line. We all know a score should be used as cue cards in rehearsal not as a script to be read. "If I were a lion tamer," the great conductor Mitropoulos once stated, "I would not enter a cage of lions reading a book entitled *How to Tame Lions*. In the same way I would not enter a rehearsal not completely prepared." Though some advocate the multicolored-highlighter-mark-everything-on-the-page approach, others feel that marking anything on the score is admitting to not studying it enough. Re-marking what is already on the page should undoubtedly be kept to the minimum necessary, however, I encourage the marking of creative ideas, relationships, discoveries or questions.

In the initial stages of studying a score I mark it with a regular black pencil. Those markings are casual, light, and simply there to remind me of things I found for use in my further and more concentrated study. At that stage, I write mostly in the bottom margin of the score or on small stick-on type notes. Markings at this time can be in prose, almost brainstorming in nature, questions for future study, remarks about something discovered, or words that will spark future ideas. Often those are more theoretical and stylistic than technical in nature.

They contain ideas about form, texture, relationships of tempo or design, contrasts of style, mutations, repetitions, development, layers of material and the like.

As I progress to studying the work in detail, I begin to use a red *erasable* pencil as well as the black pencil. My rule is to mark only what I think is complex, easily forgotten, buried in nature, or not clear-cut. Never do I suggest marking the obvious. If a work begins with a fanfare in the trumpets, it is unnecessary to mark that event. Having studied the score, that will be obvious and clear at even a basic level of understanding. A subito-forte in every part is clear and readily learned. However, a forte-piano in only the third trumpet part, buried within a complex texture of rhythmic events would be a likely item to mark.

Continuing on, the detailed study of each section of the work will yield more technical markings of chord progressions, linear movement, key relationships, articulations, bowings, special effects, dynamics, metric and tempo relationships, and tone color. When I begin to study the seams, connective tissue and the whole as a sum of its parts, the marks again become more general, stylistic and theoretical, as well as spiritual, artistic and communicative.

I seldom mark the top margin, instead reserving it for very crucial information or reminders. I always have found that writing a lot up there seemed to limit the flow of reading the score. Writing at the top of the page seems to act as a barrier, preventing eyes from looking below that space. Generally, I reserve the bottom margin of the work for ideas, thoughts, relationships, nuances of logic, and statements I wish to remember about the form, style, history, performance practice, interpretation, or rehearsing of the work. I will also express contrasting ideas that happen concurrently. For that I use a fraction such as >/- to express that some parts have accents while others are playing legato.

I use three specific markings to accentuate, highlight, or remind myself of events or ideas in the notation of the score itself: over-striking, underlining and circling. The technique of *over-striking* the printed marking in red is wonderful for such symbols as a crescendo, decrescendo, fermata, caesura, luftpause, repeat sign, and da capo. I simply write the symbol in red over the original black ink symbol. *Circling* the mark itself can reinforce small markings of dynamics and articulation. *Underlining* in red can further enhance descriptive words or phrases. This manner takes up little space and prevents a look of clutter on the score. Sometimes, though, a written word or symbol is necessary.

For example, the use of 3+2 to show metric subdivision or writing the abbreviation of an instrument just before an entrance to detail which specific instrument is playing.

I mark cues by simply using an open parenthesis at the start of the notation. The parenthesis can be made as large as necessary to include multiple voices. To stress passing tones or important single sounds, I use a circle around the notes. For longer phrases of specific importance, I use a pair of parentheses around the material. To draw attention to an event on the next page of the score, I use a variation on the old v.s. indication. Instead of writing volti subito at the bottom of the page to tell me to turn quickly, I place the v.s. marking (or the abbreviation for the instrument name) at the right margin of that instrument's line on the score. That tells me *who* on the next page needs my attention. For example, if the first measure of a page requires important attention to the third trumpet, I will place the v.s. marking (or trp.) in the right margin of the third trumpet part on the previous page of the score. In that way I am reminded exactly where to look as I turn the page.

Markings are very personal and specific to each individual. There need be no logic to your markings for anyone else. No one will ever see your markings but you. You need to understand them, use them consistently and have them be transferable through all of your work, but only in your private world. Come up with a system and language of markings that makes sense to you, is easy to use, and is clear and specific. Onward, I can smell a score just waiting to be studied!

The "Buying a House Method" of Score Study

In trying to arrive at a useful model to relate to the task of studying a score, I realized it was exactly like the process of buying a house. For those of you who have never had this experience, you should find someone who is going through this exhilarating, frustrating and overwhelming task, and tag along on a few house-hunting trips. Though this metaphor may seem trite, it is meant as a way of relating the many steps to studying a score to a non-musical real-life task. Having used this analogy often, I have seen the gleam in people's eyes when they have been empowered by a step-by-step approach that works for them. I hope this simple notion will be the catalyst for some to learn the joy and rewards that are waiting.

Step One: How Much Can You Afford? The first step in buying a house is deciding how much you can afford to spend. Through careful study of your income and expenses you can determine your price range, keeping in mind all of the other costs of buying a house such as closing fees, maintenance and insurance. This review will leave you with a price range best suited for your unique situation. As conductors, we must assess what technical and musical demands the ensemble is capable of playing. Again, we must keep in mind many facets of information. How much rehearsal time is allocated? How secure and familiar is the group with our conducting? How effective is our conducting? What other pieces will be performed? Given those factors, we can arrive at a range of difficulty suited for our ensemble.

Step Two: The Neighborhood. Once a price range has been set, you will travel to many areas that offer houses at that price level. You will visit many neighborhoods in an effort to determine which one best suits your taste and goals for your new home. There is little to be gained by looking in neighborhoods with houses well over your price range but everything to be gained by looking at every possible town or village with houses that are in that league. I don't think you would want to own the most or least expensive home in town any more than you would want to perform a work at a difficulty level of either extreme. Through careful observation you will arrive at one or two locations you really like. Finally, you will determine the neighborhood in which you wish to begin your search.

With your difficulty range in mind, we begin to look for works we wish to consider. Through listening to demonstration recordings, talking with colleagues, and attending conferences, clinics, reading sessions and concerts we can develop a broad list of works from which to choose. Do we want a piece to tax their skills at the highest level, or should this piece be technically simple enough to accomplish more musical goals? Should the piece be accessible to player and audience or should it serve to expand their stylistic horizons? Using questions such as those, we will be able to arrive at a list of characteristics the piece should possess.

Step Three: Short List. Once you decide on a price range and neighborhood, you will look at photographs of houses in an effort to arrive at a short list of homes which appeal to your taste and needs. Musically, we can arrive at a short list of works that fall into the broad category we desire.

Step Four: First Visit. You will now start to visit houses. As you drive up to each home, you immediately will get a sense of whether the house is really worth pursuing. It will strike you positively or negatively. You may see something you instantly dislike. You may see something you love. You quickly will determine whether you even want to look inside. The reasons may be tangible or indescribable. Either way, you will make an initial judgment.

That same way, we will look at the score of the first work on our short list. We will read any preface notes. Then we will start to glance at the work in an effort to get an overall view. We will read about, research and study any information available about the composer, the period, and the style of the work. We will look at any details specific to that work, such as: the reason it was written, for whom it was written, any story or narrative the composition is based upon, or if there is any preexisting material such as folksongs or hymns. We will note the general technical complexity, overt solo passages, broad divisions of form or structure, length, melodic content and style. In a short amount of time, we either will be struck by something which interests us about the work, or a feeling of indifference or dislike. Again, the reasons may be tangible or not. It doesn't matter.

Step Five: Do You Go In? If you like the house, you will decide to go in and tour the home. If you do not, you will go to the next house on your short list. You will continue that process until you see a house that strikes you. Musically, if we like the piece, we will decide to continue on and study it. If we do not, we will move to the next work on the list, repeating the process until we find a piece in which the initial glance leaves us with the feeling of wanting to pursue the work.

Step Six: I'm Ready to Get Out of My Car. You get out of your car. You stand at the curb and look at the house with a broad view. You look at it as a whole. Then, standing right there, you begin to look at the house in more detail, viewing the outside section by section, until you feel you know the outside view or parameter of the home. If you still like the house, you continue on with the process; if not, you move to the next house on the list.

As conductors, this is when we will begin formally to study the work. We will start by looking at the parameters of the work in more detail. We simply look at the piece, page by page in broad strokes. This is not the time for note-by-note detail. This is where we look at the composition for an outline, like making an outline before starting to write text. We look for large broad bits of information. Are there movements? How many movements? Are there key signatures? Does the work change key and where? What are the broad tempo indications? What is the overall emotional or expressive framework? Questions like that will leave us with an understanding of the size and broad outline of the work. If we still like the work at this juncture we go on. If not, we move to the next piece on the list.

Step Seven: I'm Ready to Go In. Armed with that outside image, you enter the house from the front door. Even if the house has sixteen outside doors, you always make your first entrance from the front door. As you enter, you stand in the foyer and look around in an effort to get perspective. Then you move at a fairly quick pace through the house in an effort to see every room and determine how the house *flows*. You move from the front door through the house until you reach the farthest point in the home. Let us say it is the back bedroom on the second floor. Once you have completed that trip through the house, you stand there for a moment and think. If you are struck with a negative opinion of the home you will move directly to the front door and exit, never looking back. If you like the house, you will begin the next step.

During score study, we will start at the first measure, studying the work, section by section. Again, we will not be looking for the minutia, but will be looking for, and filling in, information about each segment of the work. Basically, we will be adding details to the basic parameters we have already determined. We will note structural information such as section divisions, introductions, seams, bridges and themes. By reading, singing or playing parts of the work from beginning to end, we will be able to determine a rough outline of the composition. Is there an introduction? Where does the first theme begin? What is the form of the work? What are the key relationships within the harmonic structure of the work? Simply put, how does the piece move from the first note to the last?

Step Eight: Room By Room. Standing at that farthest point, after you have thought about the house for a moment, you begin to move back through the house. This time, however, you work your way through each room of the house with the most exacting detail. You notice every spot, nick, dent, crack, fault, chip or water stain. You also take note of every beautiful attribute such as the lovely molding, stunning light fixtures, etched glass windows, clean tile and polished brass heater grates. You come to know every single nail in every piece of wood. You study the good and bad of the house with unyielding focus and precision. In this portion of the study you are concentrating much more on the details of each room and much less on how they connect or relate.

As conductors, now is when we scrutinize every note and mark on the score. We start at the first note and work pitch by pitch, chord by chord, through each section. We detail important harmonic motion, rhythmic relationships, specifics of articulation, moments of tension and release, timbral shifts, passing tones, dissonances, oddities of tone color or tessitura as well as every other musical element. Again, how each section of the work relates or moves to the next is far less important now than the exacting detail of each individual section of the work. We note every problem spot as well as every beautiful nuance. We mark the score with care to highlight our revelations. We search for errors and inconsistencies as well as the joy and passion the piece has to offer. We simply must think of the words of renowned architect Mies van der Rohe: "God is in the details." As Richard Wagner put it, "The big notes come of themselves; it is the little notes that require attention...."

Step Nine: One Last Trip. Once you have studied every room of the house, you always take one last walk through the entire home. Here you want to refresh your memory of how the house flows from room to room, relate specifics of one room to others, and observe similarities and differences within the home. This is not re-examining the house, but rather taking all the information you have observed in your detailed study and making the minute particulars part of the whole.

At this point in our musical study we once again start at the first note working our way from beginning to end. As with the house, we are not interested in re-studying the details, but rather synthesizing them into how they relate and make up the whole work. How do sections flow from one to another? How is material used in one section and then used differently in another section? Does material mutate or change as it moves through the work? What similarities and differences appear? How do seams allow for motion from section to section? We must look for the odd or unusual, goal points, repetitions with subtle changes and nuances not previously caught. We must take note of contrasts and similarities.

Contrasts of timbre, dynamics, tessitura, articulation, style and the like are a remarkable source of interest. Are the contrasts simultaneous (at the same time), linear (one after the other), or staggered (one happens then is joined by another that continues after the first stops)? Look for small events often buried which would provide excitement. I call this the "blue corn" of the work. In a giant field of yellow corn the neat thing is to find one kernel of blue corn. As well, try to find what I term the "micro-styles." Even within the seeming sameness of style in a section of a work, one can find subtle differences, or micro-styles, within that style.

Contours are another source of great variety. How do shapes of line compare and contrast? Do simultaneous lines follow contours that are identical (both rise and fall at the same time), opposing (one rises as the other falls), staggered/identical (both follow the same rise and fall but start in an imitative fashion rather than at the same time) or staggered/opposing (imitative like the previous entry, however, opposing in contour)?

Step Ten: The Big Picture. Once you leave the house and walk back to your car, if you still like the house, you will do one last thing. You will stand at the curb, turn around, and take one last look at the whole picture. You will look at the entire house in one big view. This is an effort to take all the information and details you have gathered and save them in terms of the whole house. How do the parts fit into the whole? You the conductor will now glance through the score from beginning to end in a rapid, almost fleeting manner. That gives us a chance to gather a view of the whole. To truly come to understand how the parts make up the whole. To note the big picture, rather than get lost in the details.

If you start to get stumped at this point, try looking at the whole as if it were an artist's painting. Where on the canvas do things occur? Are there contrasts of high and low, foreground and background, clarity and blurring, prominence and obscurity or density and sparseness? Try using imaginary colors on an imaginary canvas in your mind. Are the flutes a faint yellow sound while the tubas are a bold dark purple? Are the trumpets bright royal blue while the percussion add moments of dense charcoal gray? Are the bassoons a warm tan while the saxophones clash with fluorescent orange? Think back to finger painting in kindergarten. Free your mind and have fun with all the musical colors of the rainbow.

Step Eleven: Sit Calmly, Think, Remember and Take Notes. After finishing your home visit or score study, you will sit comfortably in a quiet place and think about the house or score. You simply will allow your mind to wander, brainstorm, review, cogitate, stew, fester, and enjoy the memories of each moment of beauty as well as arrive at new concerns. As you come up with revelations, problems or questions you will take notes.

Step Twelve: Go Back Again. After some time has passed and a great deal of thinking has occurred, you will return to the house or score. You once again will go from beginning to end reviewing your previous information, noting new details, answering questions or concerns that arose, as well as checking the accuracy of your information and memory.

The "Jigsaw Puzzle" Approach

Another analogy I have found useful for those wanting to start to develop their score study skills is that of putting together a large, complicated jigsaw puzzle. As opposed to buying a house with that regrettable mortgage, people actually do puzzles for *fun*. Let's think about how we approach them in a manner that makes the task fruitful, enjoyable, less frustrating, and logical. First, we look at the picture on the box to gather an impression of what the *whole* looks like. In this way, we have an idea of how the entire finished product should appear. That is studying the preface materials as well as any other facts we can gather about the work. Next, we lay out every single piece of the puzzle so we can see each one. We will now have a grasp of each of the parts of the work which will come together to make the whole. That is the general overview of the composition.

After assessing the finished product and each of the component parts, we begin to assemble the puzzle by laying the perimeter of the work. We carefully select and connect each of the outside edge pieces to make the frame of the entire project. Musically, that is coming to understand the form of the work in broad strokes.

With that frame intact we begin to work on specific sections of the puzzle. Let us say that the puzzle is of a basket of fruit resting on a table. We may begin with the apple. We slowly and assuredly study each puzzle piece, segregating the apple pieces by their red color. In score study, that is equivalent to coming to understand each section of the work.

Next we are ready to assemble the apple with intricate detail. Then we move from section to section, subject by subject, securing the parts of each of those isolated topics together. That is a detailed study of each section of our composition with finite, extreme and methodical scrutiny.

With each isolated subject together it is time to study the connective tissue, seams or material that link topic sections to each other and to the whole. That may be background material, shadows, nuances of colors, or pieces that flow fluidly from one section to another. As a conductor, that is where we study the seams or connective tissue that bind each section of the work to the whole.

Once the connective or bonding material is in place, it is time to look at the whole. We note any errors, ill-fitting pieces, or ripples in the construction. That is the time to review whether the parts truly add up to the whole. Musically, we study relationships, contrasts, similarities, and the metamorphosis, development and evolution of ideas.

Then, any accomplished jigsaw-puzzle maker sits back, smoothes the surface of the puzzle and savors his or her accomplishment. As musicians, we can think about the totality of our understanding of the work. We can challenge our opinions and relish the moments of realization.

As with the analogy of buying a house, this analogy forces deductive as well as inductive reasoning. It has us work from the whole product to the parts that make it up. As well, it allows us to study how the sum of all the parts make the whole. It forces study of the minutia, the nitty-gritty, the piece by piece, as well as the flowing links between them. Those are the seams and connective tissue that make for a cohesive whole. It allows for and necessitates viewing the broad as well as the specific. Quite simply, I like to go from the big picture to the fine detail and then back to the big picture.

By studying a score this way, one examines the overview of the whole; the parameters of the whole; each section in specific detail; and the melding, mutating, conjoining and coalescing of sections. One also reassesses each of those aspects in terms of the whole product. That last notion of sitting back, looking at and thinking about the whole picture cannot be underestimated. So often in an effort to be expedient, we skip that time-consuming step. Sometimes all of our efforts to look at the minutia of details leave us with little information about the whole. The study of little facets must be tempered by an understanding of the entire object. We must look at the genesis of ideas. Where did material come from and where does it go? An understanding of a single chord or rhythmic relationship in a work is useful only when reincorporated back into an understanding of the entire composition. Thomas Stacy said it so well, "As you perform try to see the entire painting, not just the brush strokes."

This simple plan allows for a modest way of beginning the study of a score for those uncomfortable or uneasy about the task. Score study is not a one-time event. After I finish studying a work, I usually wait several months, or if possible a year, and repeat the process. It is amazing how time will allow you to see things more clearly, differently or even better. The distance of time gives you another perspective from which to study the work. You will agree with some information, revise some, and abandon some for a better way of thinking. You undoubtedly will catch little details missed in the first study of the work. As Eloise Ristad wrote in her book *A Soprano on Her Head*, "Once in a Scrabble game I had the letters B R O I N A and a blank. By using the blank as an S and using an A already available on the board I could have made the eight-letter word 'abrasion' for a modest score, with a fifty point bonus for using all seven letters. But the free A disappeared before my turn. My mind was so stuck on the word 'abrasion' that I almost missed the possibility of juggling my letters one more time, using the blank as a W and making the word 'rainbow.' I ended up with a triple-word score on rainbow, plus forming two extra words along the way, plus my fifty point bonus for going out. It was a perfectly obvious move once I turned loose of my first word and played around with new possibilities for the blank. But the word 'abrasion' was a long way from the word 'rainbow.' It took the juggling — the act of disorienting myself, disengaging myself from the orderliness of the first word I discovered — to find a new word. I had a sense of commitment to my first word, and a sense of loss when it disappeared from the realm of possibility that all but prevented me from going beyond it. The word 'abrasion' was not wrong; it simply no longer fit the Scrabble board." As Georg Christoph Lichtenberg so eloquently reminds us, "There is a great difference between still believing something and believing it again." Without question, time away from the study of the composition provides mental space or solace, freedom to quietly think without pressure, and time to relax with and mull over a work, which can yield great results.

After each rehearsal we also will have a prime opportunity to revisit our study of the work. Through rehearsing the work and detailing an errata for the composition, we will change opinions, find additional details, have new revelations and come to know the piece in differing ways. Take a few moments soon after the end of a rehearsal to decompress, review the rehearsal, and think about your conducting as well as the score. It is an invaluable time that should be cherished and preserved at all costs. I truly believe it can be the most fruitful and enjoyable time in that details are fresh in one's mind. Even a few minutes are worth their weight in gold.

Now, go on! What are you waiting for? Open the cupboards or look under the living room couch or wherever you stash your scores and try that straightjacket on for size. ▨

BUT HOW DO I GET THEM TO WATCH?

I'd like you to close your eyes and picture a place. A remarkable place. There, you live in a beautiful house. You have wonderful neighbors. There are great schools. There are no taxes. You can eat anything you want. Everything there is free and your opinion is law. Picture such a place. Can you imagine how happy you would be living there? Wouldn't it be fabulous? But, there is one problem — that place is on Mars, there is no oxygen, and you would die.

To me, that scenario is just like conducting. Though it may seem absolutely ridiculous, think about it for a moment. No matter how developed our conducting skills are, no matter how much we polish our technique as a conductor, if our students don't watch that conducting, it is all for naught. I don't know the answer to the age-old question, "If a tree falls in the woods and there is no one there to hear it, does it make a sound?" I will leave that to those far more learned than I, but I do know that if a conductor makes the greatest gesture or facial expression and there is no one watching, it doesn't mean a darn thing!

I believe our purpose as a conductor is to present a logical, consistent, causative and meaningful nonverbal language that emulates sound in motion so that our ensemble can perform that sound. The glaring necessity in that sentence is the players must be *watching* that language as presented by the conductor. We can conduct the most perfect subito-piano gesture, but if no one is watching us, it is meaningless. For nonverbal language to be effective it must be observed. In that case, a tree that falls in the woods when no one is there to hear it positively *does not* make a sound. Simply by changing certain attitudes, perspectives and techniques we *can* get an ensemble to diligently watch us.

Through that, we can communicate every aspect of our interpretation, improve discipline and thoroughly engage students in rehearsals.

For that to happen effectively, I think of conducting in terms of what I call *The Conducting Cycle.* I believe this four-step approach offers a way to view each part of the process of how we develop and communicate as conductors. Each step in this cycle is predicated on the steps that come before it. First, we develop our technical ability to conduct gestures. If we think of this as learning a foreign language, it would be where we develop a large working knowledge of vocabulary words and how to use them correctly. As conductors, at this stage we must hone our skills to become confident in our ability to convey technical information as well as impressionistic feelings about music. That is like building a giant glossary of conducting gestures and techniques and tucking them away in our heads. Until we have developed our conducting technique, I think it is less than fruitful to try to apply gestures to a composition. To me, it would be like asking a young person learning a language to write a story before he or she had learned a sufficient number of vocabulary words to use in the creation of that story.

Secondly, we must study the work we want to conduct to the point of having a true understanding of it. Simply put, we must know the score cold. Then, thirdly, we apply that glossary of conducting techniques to the score we have studied. Here we take abstract gestures that convey specific meaning to an ensemble and appropriately apply those gestures to the music as a result of our study. The last step is to train the ensemble to watch the conductor well enough to receive that information. If we are going to use that nonverbal communication we call conducting in our rehearsals, we have to get them to watch.

Without a doubt, the most common question I receive from teachers is, "How do you get the players to watch?" Interesting, isn't it? It is never: "I don't have any idea how I want that section to sound," or "I don't know what emotion I want to express here." Never. We all know what we want musically. We have that running around in our souls and hearts. The question is always how to get the ensemble to watch so we can express that which we have within us.

I am now going to share the answer to that question with you. Ready? It's going to be earth-shattering. Though it is longwinded and extremely complicated, here it goes. (Can you hear the drum roll?) Hold on tight. The answer — *you give them no other choice!* At this moment, you must be thinking, "You're kidding right, that's it?" I am sorry. The answer is so simple, but nevertheless true. But it goes beyond insisting, cajoling, asking, mandating, or ordering them to watch us. It is more in the realm of drawing them in to you, focusing them on you, attracting their minds, and in short making them almost magnetically pulled toward your being. For any age ensemble, it is using the power of your personality. Though that may sound like a load of psycho-babble, we only need be present at a rehearsal by a conductor who has that power to realize its ability to communicate with an almost mesmerizing quality. With that as our goal, let's talk about how we can go about getting them to watch.

Give Them Something Meaningful To Watch

We must make certain that when students look at us, they see truly meaningful communication. How often are our rehearsal rooms filled with the sound of us saying, "watch me" or "look up?" If students then look up and see nothing meaningful, why would they look up the next time that is said? Even more importantly, why would they look up at times when they are not chided to do so? They would simply think, "Why should I watch, there's nothing to see." That is the single biggest problem we have in getting players to watch. Picture watching a television set, that as a result of being broken, has no picture. It is a blank screen. A voice from the set says, "Look up." You look up only to see a blank screen. Discouraged, you look away. Again, you hear the same words from the television. You look up. Again, you see a blank screen and look away frustrated. As this goes on for ten or twenty times, you grow angry and frustrated. You also stop looking at the set when you hear those words. That's what happens when we ask performers to look at us and all they see is our beating time.

If, however, we provide meaningful communication when students look at us, we reinforce that "watching" behavior and encourage them to repeat it. A helpful cue or perfectly understood fermata motivates students to watch for more. Communicating a stimulating crescendo will make performers want to make that connection to you again and again. They got something from looking up, so they will be inclined to do so again. That would be like our hearing the voice from that television set asking us to look up, but this time we see a vibrant, multicolored image. Now we will want to look up as much as possible. It becomes self-perpetuating and self-reinforcing.

You Watch Them

We constantly must be looking at our performers, all of them, not just principal players or soloists, every last one of them. To that end, we can't be buried in the score. We can't, as Warren Benson said, be playing "musical water-polo," constantly bobbing up and down as if gasping for breath in an effort to read the score as we glance fleetingly at them. If every time players look up at the podium they see their conductor looking at the score, they soon will realize they need not look up. Conductors whose eyes are not constantly on their players are almost guaranteeing the players will cease watching them. Conversely, if when looking up they see your face and your eyes, students will have had a meaningful experience. They will want to look again.

Make It Matter

I am convinced students watch when they know it matters. Our goal must be to make it matter to every one of them. Let me tell you a story to try to explain myself. Traveling from my home to the university, I drive a rather complicated and circuitous route through many housing developments in an effort to avoid traffic. I have driven that same path every day for years. At several intersections along the way there are stop signs. And though I stop, I do so in a very casual manner because the area is always deserted. In a decade, I have yet to see a single car or person there. A few years ago, as I pulled up to one of those stop signs, I saw a police officer watching intently while sitting in his car off to the side of the intersection. I came to a profound stop. Remembering back to my driver's education class, I counted to ten. Actually, not remembering how long you're supposed to count, I counted to twenty just to be safe! I waved hello to the officer and continued.

The next day, as I pulled up to that stop sign, I saw the police car. Again, I stopped with great emphasis, counted sincerely, waved adamantly and then moved on. That policeman made it matter that I look at him. I knew he was watching me. That went on for about four days.

You know what? That was eight years ago. I have never seen a police car at that intersection again, but always, and I mean always, I watch for him. Even more, I watch for him at every other stop sign on that remote route just in case he's watching. By watching me he made it matter, and even though I may never see him again, I always look, just on the off chance he's watching me. If every time students look up at the podium, they see your eyes, they will realize that you are watching them. All of a sudden, it will then matter to them just like the watchful eye of the policeman mattered to me. We just have to make it matter to all of our students. Performers watch when they know you're looking at them. It matters.

Positive Reinforcement For Watching

We need to "convert" every student into a believer! We must convince them how important it is to watch. Though the success of good musical communication between performer and conductor is extremely reinforcing, I believe we should go even farther. In an effort to convert every student into becoming a watcher, the use of verbal positive reinforcement cannot be underestimated. Paraphrasing the words of Kenneth Blanchard and Spencer Johnson, we need to catch them doing something *right*! Then, when we see that they are watching, all we need to do is offer a simple compliment: a "thank you" to people for following so well, a "great eyes" to a player for looking at us.

Equally important are nonverbal positive reinforcements such as a wink, nod, smile, okay sign or thumbs up to clearly show our appreciation for, as well as reinforce those watching behaviors. Those gestures work remarkably well to reward positive behaviors. But more importantly, because they are nonverbal communications, they in and of themselves reinforce watching. To receive that praise students must be *looking for,* rather than *listening for,* the reward. I use those gestures all the time. I believe them to be the single best method of getting performers to watch. Let's face it, we all want a pat on the back. We all respond to praise by repeating the behavior that originally got us praise.

The process of getting an ensemble to watch is a slow one. We really have to do it one person at a time. However, once it is cultivated, it is long lasting. Psychology tells us that even an intermittent reward, one that comes infrequently and unpredictably, is a very strong reinforcement. Once our students feel the success generated by watching, and experience those positive verbal and nonverbal rewards, they will become addicted to watching for the long haul.

My favorite experience in trying to get an ensemble to watch was at a middle school band festival some years ago. During the course of the three days of rehearsals, I did everything I am advocating in this chapter. One by one, I got each of them hooked on watching. All, that is, except one saxophone player. I tried everything. I dug down so deep in my bag of tricks that I hit the floor. Nothing worked. I could not get him to look up. I talked, begged, pleaded, reprimanded. Still, nothing worked. I knew all I needed to do was get him to look at me one time. Just one time and I could use positive reinforcement to reward his efforts enough that he would want to watch. Time passed and it just wasn't going to happen. By that point his lack of watching, with an ensemble that was watching intently, was causing havoc. I had to do something drastic.

So in the middle of rehearsing a passage, I abruptly stopped the group. Pointing right at this young man, I energetically said, "I'm sorry I had to stop, but I just had to tell this young man how incredible his watching has been. If everyone watched like he did, I can't imagine how it would sound!" Well, yes, depending on your semantic interpretation, I lied. As I said the words, that fellow sat nine feet taller in his chair and smiled from ear to ear. I then started to rehearse again. That young boy didn't blink, let alone look down at his music, for the rest of the weekend. It worked. At that moment he realized watching would be rewarded. When it comes to getting an ensemble to watch, I don't think as human beings we are much different than Skinner mice! Rewarding positive behavior works. Just ask that little saxophonist!

Negative Identification

This is a two-part technique that does work; however, the second part of it is what makes it work. So you must promise to read the next entry, for this technique *alone* is far too negative to be useful. It goes like this. When I have a student not looking up, I will hold my left arm fully extended, pointing directly at him, staring directly into his eyes while I continue to conduct with my right hand. I allow this to go on for a short while. Then when the student finally looks up and sees my index finger pointing at him, he is truly startled. Continuing to conduct, still looking at him, I use my left hand now to point to my own eyes and shake my head from side to side with a disappointed look on my face. No words are spoken. Now, you may be wondering what if that student doesn't ever look up to see your pointing finger? Then I stop the ensemble as I continue to point. Usually, students look up at that moment and see my index finger. I then point to my eyes, shake my head and frown. If anything, I will simply say, "I've been pointing at you for the past twenty measures." That's it, nothing more. Now that brings us to the most important part of this technique.

The Little Man On My Shoulder

I believe we each have a little, tiny, miniature person sitting on our shoulder. They are a perfect replica of us. They are ever present. For me, he is the filter through which everything goes before I speak. He instantly determines what is acceptable and beneficial, and what is hurtful and useless. He is my conscience, my better self, my rational guide and the wiser person I want to be. He also must have a perfect memory. The vast majority of his job is to remember exactly with whom I have used negative identification. For if negative identification is to work, it absolutely must be followed with positive reinforcement. After having used negative identification, I continue to rehearse, incessantly watching that person.

Undoubtedly, after that finger-pointing episode, he will look up at least once. My job now must be to basically stare at him, waiting to catch him looking, and reward him 'til the cows come home. When he does look up, I will stare right at his face, use my left index finger to point to my eyes, nod my head up and down while smiling as big as the sun. Then my left hand will either make an okay sign or the thumbs up sign aimed right at him. I try to make it abundantly clear that though I had to "point out" the negative behavior, I am far more delighted to reward the positive behavior. The trick is that the little person on my shoulder can never forget. Never.

Cue Incessantly

Though cueing is really part of offering meaningful communication, I mention it here because I believe that cueing as often as possible is one of the easiest and best ways to develop watching and the communicative visual dialogue with which it goes. Cueing allows us to spend a great deal of time watching students while at the same time offering them meaningful communication. I am firmly convinced that the more a conductor cues, the more a group watches.

Eradicate Obstacles

Though each of the preceding ideas will help train students to watch the conductor, they will do little if obstacles are present that prevent or hinder students from watching. The impediments to communication, discussed in another chapter, such as poles, sunlight, ramp rails and the dead zone for seating all have great impact. Years ago, a band director friend of mine asked me to work with his band. He wanted some help in getting them to watch better. As we began the rehearsal, I saw why they didn't watch. They couldn't. It was physically impossible. There was an upright piano blocking the view of many people, a percussion section so far behind the back of the group as to be in a different zip code, risers creating angles that forced some players to face away from the conductor, and a third of the ensemble behind or to the side of the conductor in the dead zone. My guess is that all in all only about twenty percent of the ensemble could actually see the face of the conductor. That is a formula for frustration.

Obstacles come in many guises. They can be anything and anywhere. We must be ever vigilant in our awareness of them, and alter our set-up so as to make them moot. The bottom line is that sometimes when players aren't watching us it's because they can't. So before I have that immediate urge to think that players aren't watching me because they are having a nervous breakdown, suffering from temporary insanity or inferior genes, I check to see if they actually can see me.

I truly believe chairs and music stands can be two of the biggest obstacles we must contend with. If our rows of chairs are set to place each player's head directly behind the person in the row ahead of him, we will spend that rehearsal watching every player stretch his head and neck to the side so as to make it possible to see the podium. If we simply stagger each row of chairs by half a chair's distance, we solve the problem. In that way, a player's head is lined up to see between the two chairs in the row in front of him. Now with the aid of a podium placed well in *front* of the ensemble to increase the conductor's visibility, the problem is solved.

With regard to music stands, I sometimes think they may be our worst enemy! They unquestionably don't help the situation. First, let's talk about the conductor's stand. Obviously, we want our stand as low and unobtrusive as possible. We certainly don't want to hit it or have it block a student's view of us. With that said (and the knowledge that I am about to bang headfirst into some people's deeply held convictions) I also am not an advocate of having the conductor's stand flat with the angled ledge facing toward the ensemble. Though that common approach does get the stand low and out of view, it also sets up what I call a vertical tennis match. If the stand is kept as low as possible and parallel to the ground, unless the conductor's eyesight is very odd, the only way to see the score will be to stand directly above it, lean over, curl our back forward and look straight down. That sets up the vertical tennis match whereby we bob up and down from looking at the score to the players like the audience at a tennis match watches the ball move from side to side. If however, we keep the stand low and angled in the traditional way, we can stay well behind the stand with no bending, curling or leaning. All the while we can keep our head and eyes aimed forward rather than down.

I simply keep my stand as low as possible, with a steep angle, setting the height by placing my left finger tips in the far right lower corner of the stand as if turning pages. In that way I don't have to walk closer, bend over or otherwise alter my stance to turn a page or look at the players. It is easy, free and not cumbersome in anyway. With that steep angle, I can stay well behind the stand, making it almost impossible to hit the stand with my hands or baton, and can maintain a visual line-of-sight angle that is conducive to constantly looking at the players.

When it comes to music stands for our players, I am a firm believer in keeping them as high as possible. I ask them to set the stand height so that when they lift their eyes just above the music, they are looking into my face. In that way, they need not bob their heads up and down, but simply move their eyes. In addition, I feel a stand height of that nature helps promote good embouchures, breathing and posture.

Now if my panning a flat conductor's stand didn't get you, this next one will. I am a firm believer in not sharing stands. Whenever possible, I try to have a stand for each person. Why? Think about it. When we ask two people to share a stand, their direct line of sight is now angled. One player is looking to his left while one player is looking to his right. If the players are in front of the conductor that's not so bad, however, if the players are to one side, one of them is forced to look away from the conductor to see the music. That certainly does not promote the idea of popping their eyes above the stand and seeing my face!

One last obstacle I need to mention is the score. Though it can be our guide to discovering the wonders of a work, and help us teach young people to accomplish great things, it is also a treacherous obstacle. It is like an addictive drug. It calmly and subtly lures us into feeling we are reliant on it and need it. It's like a security blanket. If we read it and focus on it, we will never get performers to watch. Whether it's turning pages awkwardly or being buried in it, the score can be a vicious deceiver.

Insistence

Once they can see us, we need simply to insist that they watch. In other words, we leave them no possibility other than to watch. We give them no other option. This should start when we teach conducting gestures in warm-up exercises. By teaching them the meaning of each isolated gesture they will learn our nonverbal language like vocabulary words. Using scales, chords, canons, and unison tones without reading music, students will have nothing to look at but you. They can focus all of their attention on your communication. During that time we can use all the aforementioned techniques to foster and reward watching. The situation is basically rigged to succeed!

After gestures are understood and become meaningful in warm-up exercises, we can transfer their use into musical compositions. At that transfer point, our insistence becomes crucial. We must now contend with the printed music drawing their eyes away from us. We must be evangelical in our efforts to keep them watching. Though that task may seem overwhelming, we can think of it in three areas. First, we must insist on precise initial attacks. We can't let them accept a sloppy or ruffled attack. We didn't in our warm up exercises, so why should we now? Once an ensemble proves they can perform a perfect initial attack, we must insist upon nothing less — always. Students must understand our expectations. A sloppy starting attack sets the tone for inattentive playing. Conversely, the sure footing provided by a solid initial attack acts as a springboard for their continued watching, focus and precision.

Secondly, we must insist they stop with us instantly. We must teach them that the group stops playing the moment we stop conducting. I tell my students that if they play on for three measures, it means they haven't looked up for three measures. Conversely, in that I ask them to check-in with me at least once a measure in a moderately paced work, they should all stop within that "one measure" amount of time. Allowing them to play on wastes rehearsal time, but more importantly fosters an unspoken condoning of them not watching. As well, I think this may be the truest use of the adage "Give them an inch and they will take a mile." If we allow a bit of playing on, it will slowly increase until it is out of hand. I think we have to be firm and insistent. I use phrases such as, "I stopped three measures ago," or "I stopped at letter D." I try to be calm and refined, but show my displeasure at this unacceptable practice. Positive reinforcement can be of help here as well. I often suggest rigging a spot in a piece at the beginning of a rehearsal where you know you can get them to stop instantly with you, so as to be able to praise it highly. We need to get them used to the sound of an attentive stop in rehearsals.

Insisting on a perfect initial attack is certainly the easiest first step. Insisting on an instant stop is the next easiest. Once they are fairly consistent with those, we must begin to be as insistent with other conducting gestures used within a work. So the third aspect of this insistence is *that if we conduct it, they must play it.* If you conduct a crescendo, they must follow. If you execute a forte-piano they must as well. Though that sounds pretty obvious, I feel that no gesture can go without being responded to by the ensemble. As long as we check to be certain our conducting is sound, we must require the performance of every gesture. It's that kind of insistence that will convince an ensemble they must actually watch. Conversely, if we allow an ensemble to ignore our gestures, we are reinforcing the fact that they don't need to watch us in the first place.

Though it may sound strange, I think of this like breaking a horse. It is constant insistence on the task at hand, the unwavering strength of not letting the horse change the task or your expectations, and your willingness to persevere. The horse will soon learn that no matter how hard it tries to make you give up, you will continue demanding the expected behavior. Finally, through firm, kind, appropriate, calm and sincere control of the situation, the horse will give in to your wishes. Another example I use is that of a parent disciplining a child. The frustrating part of that task is saying the same thing over and over. After Billy hits his sister for the hundredth time, and you have corrected him for the hundredth time, at the next occurrence, there is always the thought of just ignoring the behavior. We can't. It is the constant and continuous attention to that behavior which will teach Billy it is unacceptable. So we can't ignore that crescendo our students didn't perform, because it probably means they didn't see us conduct it. And if they didn't see it, it probably means they weren't watching.

Throughout this process, we won't tell the ensemble that they are wrong, but that they are not doing what we are communicating in our hands. Statements like, "That's not what my hands are doing," or "That's not what my hands look like," clearly state the problem as a lack of communication rather than only an error in performance.

Never Let Them Win

Boy that sounds harsh, doesn't it? I don't mean they shouldn't be free to express opinions, ask questions or offer valuable input during rehearsals. What I mean is that they can't take control of the situation. If we start a work at a certain tempo only to find the ensemble moves at a slower tempo, we can't give in. We can't go with them. We must make them come with us. In short, we can't let them win. If we conduct a *suddenly* slower change of tempo, and they collectively perform a ritardando, we have two choices. We can give in to their pressure and manipulation, or stay our ground and force them to follow our tempo. Though it may be easier to join them than to fight them, if we do, they will quickly learn they can win. If that happens, the necessity for them to watch is gone. True, there are times when it's not worth the fight. But unfortunately, we can't hold up a sign as we conduct which reads, "I really mean it this time!"

Once students learn they can't win, they usually give up trying to *win*, and focus their efforts on watching you. Years ago someone told me that was the same approach used to keep an elephant from wandering away. Greatly puzzled, I asked him to explain. Did you ever wonder how a giant elephant is secured when he is standing out in a field at the circus? He is held by a chain that is pinned into the ground. Yep, a chain not much bigger than you would use for your dog Fido. How can that work? That elephant could move a car let alone a chain. The gentleman said a baby elephant is secured just that way when he is tiny (if you can use that word for an elephant). The elephant endlessly tries to pull up that chain. He can't. So he stops trying and becomes resigned to that chain holding him there. As the elephant grows bigger and bigger he doesn't bother trying to break the chain because he remembers back when he couldn't get it to budge. The elephant doesn't realize that he could now snap the chain with one good tug. Once your students realize they can't budge you from your intent, like the elephant, they will stop trying to do so.

The Diet Syndrome

Sadly, I have done more than my fair share of dieting. So often the first day of my diet goes like this: I wake up that morning and have nothing but coffee. I go to work, and there in the office is a box of donuts. With my willpower firmly in place, I walk by them with determination and have another cup of coffee. An hour or so later I go to the office for something and see those donuts again. Full of conviction, I pass them by on my way to another cup of coffee. That goes on all morning. By about noon, I go into the office and there I see that broken-off piece of donut (that by law someone must leave in the box). My will power now drained, I think to myself, "What would one tiny little piece hurt?" I reach in the box and joyously eat that morsel. At that moment I immediately think, "That's it, the diet is shot, so I might as well go to the student union and eat a whole pizza or three." I call this *The Diet Syndrome*. The odd logic that makes this so debilitating is thinking, "Since the diet was broken, it really doesn't matter how badly I break it from then on."

I believe when it comes to watching, especially regarding stopping with us, ensembles function much the same way. Rehearsals often start with students very motivated to watch, diligently stopping with the conductor. As time goes on they maintain that focus. Then for no apparent reason they stop watching and start to play on. Rather than simply regrouping, redoubling their efforts and going back to the task at hand, the rehearsal starts to become less than productive and controlled. In their collective minds, once they stopped being attentive for even that one moment, it really doesn't matter how badly they act from then on. We must stop that chain-reaction. When it does break down, we need to nip it in the bud. We must reset their attention. We must reinforce their progress and accomplishments. Even if we need to go back to a warm-up exercise to have them play something accurately *with us,* it is worth the time to center their concentration and focus, so as not to lose the rest of that rehearsal to the diet syndrome.

Try To Fool Them

I know you are thinking, "That old trick?" It is as old as the hills, but it really does work. You know, when the conductor makes a giant preparation, but freezes in midair rather than give the initial attack of the work, or adds ritards to a piece where they never had been? As silly as it seems, I really think it works. It is a great way to test whether they are watching or not. If our communication doesn't work, it provides a lighthearted moment of levity, but when it does work, it offers us a wonderful chance for positive reinforcement.

Another wonderful way of assessing how well they are watching is to videotape a rehearsal. Aiming the camera at the players' faces very quickly tells us when they are, and who is, watching. It clearly identifies the quantity and quality of our ensemble's eye contact with us. Placing the camera so it is aimed directly at our eyes objectively tells us the quantity and quality of *our* eye contact with the ensemble.

Playing A Spot By Memory

I think that half of the process of getting an ensemble to watch is to convince them they don't need to be glued to the printed page of music. To that end, I often will run to one side of the rehearsal room, toward the back of the ensemble. I will then tell them all to turn around, look at me, and play by memory a spot in the work we are rehearsing. They always grimace and say they can't. After they do it, almost always extremely well, I use that to try to convince them they don't need those fuzzy black dots on the white page. After a while, they learn that their brain has it all in there ready to go!

Aural Cues

If you were part of a large group of people gathered in a room I would demonstrate this topic. I would ask all of you to close your eyes and not open them until I specifically told you to do so. After giving you a starting pitch, I would say, "Sing quarter notes with me — one, two, ready, play." After a few measures of that, I would ask the men to get louder, the ladies to get softer, those with red hair to accent every note, those with brown eyes to sing molto legato. I would then say, "Everyone slow down — two, three, four," as I slowed my chanting of the pitches. Then clapping loudly as I increased the speed, I would say, "faster — two, three, four." After a few more measures, I would click my baton repeatedly on the stand and tell you to stop.

I then would tell you to look up at me. What you would see are my hands held above my head locked into bright blue handcuffs. They are plastic and stupid looking, but they profoundly illustrate how insidiously awful aural cues are to the process of getting an ensemble to watch the conductor. We would have just completed a five-minute rehearsal. During that time I would have gotten you to start, increase and decrease tempo, change articulation, and stop. All the while, keeping your eyes closed. The snapping, clapping, tapping, and counting off of that aural rehearsal completely replaced the need for anyone to watch the conductor. In that aural cues are initially more accessible than those that are nonverbal, players will respond to aural cues and basically ignore nonverbal ones. Aural cues negate the need to watch the conductor. They basically reinforce the notion that as a player I can bury my head in the music, never look up, and get all the information I need to perform the work with the ensemble.

I'm the first to admit that aural cues are easy to use and do get results. They are like refined sugar. That sweet ingredient is extremely alluring. However, a steady diet of it would probably kill you. I think of the decision to use aural cues like choosing a path to a far off location. Using aural cues is the path that has no hills and is very smooth, but leads you miles away from your goal. Choosing not to use them is like taking a path with a few steep climbs that is rocky at times, but is the shortest and most direct route to your goal.

The Conductor/Ensemble Relationship

The tangible and intangible attributes necessary to become an effective conductor are many and varied. We could go on for hours about the qualities of personality that make for a wonderful conductor. Though developing that conducting persona is important, I think even more important is the development of the conductor/ensemble relationship. That nearly indescribable, interactive and interpersonal transmission of attitudes and perceptions between performers and conductor is the foundation of powerful musical communication.

The key to that relationship is what I call: *Trust, Require and Reliance.* The first aspect is trust. Have you ever been to a party where they had you close your eyes and fall backward into the *supposedly* waiting arms of the rest of the group of people? You stand there afraid at the prospect of falling and not being caught, but finally you decide to give it a try. You lean back and hope. To your thrill and amazement, you actually did land in the arms of your friends. That is trust. It is not trust that you are sure will work, but it is trust nonetheless. In that situation, if you are going to do it, you have no choice but to trust. There is no other option. That is what we can do for our players. We can conduct a warm-up exercise or even a single note and give them no choice but to watch us. We insist they watch, give them meaningful information, and reward that effort. With no music in front of them, they have no other place to look. If they know we are prepared, dedicated and concerned they will grow to trust us.

Once trust is established, then practiced and reinforced it then can become *required*. I tell groups that once they play one beautiful initial attack with me, that is all that will be accepted. I truly mean it. Any initial attack from that point on, which is less than acceptable is redone. They quickly learn that I will insist on them watching at all times. I don't yell or scream. I simply insist. You can't let down for a moment in those initial rehearsals at that crucial time in the development of this relationship. You require that they watch. Simply put, you require that they play what you are conducting.

After a great deal of time requiring this new found trust, one day in rehearsal you will all of a sudden realize that not only do they trust you enough to follow you and are indeed following you, but that they have become *reliant* upon you. They can't play as well without your conducting. You, or better put, your conducting has made them better than themselves. Though they could play an initial attack fairly well without you, with your hands it is pristine. Their forte-piano is good when you are not conducting, but it is vibrantly precise with your hands in motion. You have gotten them so used to watching you for every detail of playing that they need you. That is the goal. It is a frightening one to consider. A conductor who is ignored most of the time by players who at best let the gestures not mess them up, has it fairly easy. The performers don't expect anything, not much is provided, and both go happily along. The group will basically play as well as the group can play. They might as well write "DLU" at the top of each page of music. You know, that acronym for "Don't Look Up," used by many players as a reminder that the conductor is more harm than help at that point in the music. It is a shorthand way of noting the music would be better served by them staring at their parts rather than risk being confused by the conductor. Though it's sad, it is also true.

Contrast that to an ensemble that has become reliant on their conductor. They look to you to make them shine, to be better than they can be without you, to make the ensemble greater than just the sum of the parts. They look to you for everything. They scrutinize and watch for every gesture. The frightening aspect of this is that if you err, they will err. If you falter, they will falter. So, you ask why strive for this goal? Why not follow the old advice of the cartoon where on a music stand are the directions for a conductor, telling one to pick up stick, wave hands in the air, and bow when the music stops? Why? Because on the positive side, when they ascend to heights of beauty, you will have been the catalyst. When they execute a passage with precision, it will be your intent. When they reach out with sounds that scream of passion, or cry of anguish, you will have set them free to truly emote. They will be one with you. They will be the best of you. You will truly be their conductor. You will make them better than themselves.

That last phrase, to me, is what it's all about. That is, and has always been my personal goal. I wish I could take credit for it, however, it is paraphrased from the words of Hugo Burghauser describing the reaction of players of the Vienna Philharmonic after their first performance with Arturo Toscanini. Burghauser, who was the first bassoonist as well as President of the orchestra, stated that this was the "...climax of every musician's experience. Not only because he was superior to other conductors—which was taken for granted; but because he made us *superior to ourselves*—which was the phenomenon that was practically unexplainable." By having your players become addicted to watching, and reliant upon you to foster their success, you will seal and cement a conductor/ensemble relationship that will indeed become a practically unexplainable phenomenon.

Player Responsibility Versus Conductor Responsibility

The last few pages undoubtedly lead to the question of who is responsible for the ensemble's performance. This may be the single hottest and most argued topic of recent years. On one end of the continuum are those who believe that the students are responsible for every aspect of the rehearsal. To them, the conductor is only a *facilitator.* They will not *tell* players anything, but rather guide conversations between players so as to have them discuss all matters of their performance. The other extreme being those who feel the conductor is responsible for all aspects of the performance. They believe there can only be one interpretation at any given rehearsal, and it is theirs. Though they will certainly ask for student feedback, discuss possible choices in interpretation, and allow for personal renderings of solo passages, they foster more in the way of dogmatic instructions. Though the rehearsal is far more conductor centered, he or she is always compassionate, firm, sincere, and approachable. Every student knows his or her conductor is unequivocally committed to high expectations, grand achievements and exposing the great beauty of music, but is equally and unyieldingly devoted to caring about students.

Please don't think for a minute that I am describing the approach I call the ruthless dictator. That approach, common years ago, uses personal attacks, often having little to do with the music, as a means to an end. Those conductors believe they must rule with an iron fist and a cruel tongue. Fear is the catalyst of their rehearsals. It goes well beyond being strict or firm. It is more in the manner of belittling and despising. A ruthless dictator's rehearsal has comments like: "You are an idiot, why are you single handedly ruining *my* performance? You would do us much less harm sitting in the audience. *You* are awful." They rarely state what was wrong with the playing, or how to correct it, but usually dwell on attacking the person. Through that intimidation they feel they get students "playing on the edge of their chairs." Though I am sure they have the best of intentions, and often arrive at a fine performance, I can't believe the negatives don't outweigh the positives when control goes to that extreme.

The facilitator's rehearsal goes something like this: "Flutes, how do you think the trumpets just played measure seventeen?" As the flutes begin to respond to the teacher they are interrupted with statements like, "Don't look at me, tell them." "I think it was too soft," says one flute while another chimes in with "I think it was too loud." The facilitator then asks the trumpets to play that spot at a softer volume, then again at a louder dynamic level. Then the facilitator asks the flutes to debate those performances. After that, other players are queried about the trumpets' interpretation. That goes on for every aspect of the performance. The players slowly arrive at a group *consensus* interpretation. Conversely, those who feel the conductor is totally responsible for the rehearsal would have that same scenario go like this, "Trumpets, measure seventeen is too loud; it should be piano."

No doubt the facilitator will help students develop the skill of arriving at an interpretation and allow them to take ownership of the process as well as the product. Both of those goals are admirable. However, I think they can be better served through the coaching of solo and ensemble works. The time needed to truly facilitate all aspects of a large-ensemble composition is enormous. As well, I question whether students have the necessary preparation with regard to music history, theory and ear training to allow for a learned interpretation. Do they know what level of achievement is possible, and how best to get there? I agree with the words of Michael Gorman, who said, "A student by definition is a person who doesn't know what he or she doesn't know."

Clearly, I fall firmly on the side of conductor responsibility. I believe we must be the guide, the person who sets and raises the bar, the person possessing the knowledge necessary to help them reach their goals. Undoubtedly, using a bit of both approaches may be best. Surely, our innate personalities will have a lot to do with what comes most naturally to us.

Either approach, and everywhere in between, can be extremely effective. Though I don't feel the role of facilitator is always the best way, I think it can be extremely valuable, as long as it is truly what is believed as the best approach by the conductor and is not being used because it is more comfortable for them. By that I mean we must guard against it becoming a rationalization for undeveloped or weak conducting technique, a lack of conductor preparedness, or not wanting to extend the effort to get the ensemble to watch.

If our technique is weak, it is easier to talk about a release than give it clearly. If we are less than prepared, it is easier to discuss a passage than give fervent directions for its improvement. If our ensemble doesn't watch, it is easier to have them arrive at a tempo they like than to teach them to watch well enough to take our tempo. If we really believe in the facilitator role, that's great. I just hope it is not used because it is easier to unload the responsibility onto players than to develop our communication and technique so we can assume that responsibility. I remember listening to a facilitator/conductor at a rehearsal once say to his ensemble, "The piece just fell apart. It's not my fault. If you want it to be good, you will keep it from falling apart. It's up to you." The students are made completely responsible for the ensemble's progress and achievement, as well as its interpretation. I am just not sure that is the best way. My admonition to every ensemble I conduct is if they are looking at me, I'll take responsibility for everything. I tell them that even if the roof caves in, or the sun explodes, if they are watching me, it is my fault. For if they are watching, I can be of help. Without their eyes I am useless.

I think we *need* to take control of our rehearsals and insist they watch us. Not through mean-spiritedness, but through firm persistence. We must develop our conducting technique to be truly proficient and communicative, so we offer meaningful communication. We must be prepared, coming to rehearsals with a reasoned, learned, researched opinion. We must get them to watch so that we can guide them through our interpretation. Our rehearsal style must have us ready to correct errors and offer constructive criticism. We must be so "on top of things" as to be ahead of our players and anticipate their mistakes! But most of all we can help lead them to a performance so powerful and beautiful that they cherish those results and the work needed to get there.

One Final Thought

By now, I hope you are not saying to yourself that all of this getting them to watch sounds great, but is impossible. To that I can only respond with the words of a Chinese proverb I found in a fortune cookie many years ago: "Every truly great accomplishment is at first impossible." It is a long, sometimes frustrating road. It is also a path that leads to wondrous things.

EFFECTIVE REHEARSAL COMMUNICATION

The night before I gave a workshop using this title for the very first time, I was sitting in the band room with a group of my graduate students. We had just finished a rehearsal and were talking about a myriad of topics. One of them asked me where I was off to in the coming weeks. I told him I was leaving for Germany for some conducting and to present a workshop. They asked which session I was giving. I told them it was a new one. As with all of my new titles, I have always felt the need to run them by my wife and graduate students for validation. How's that for secure? They dutifully asked what the title was. I told them it was "Effective Rehearsal Communication For The Conductor." They decided it was a pretty dumb title. I defended my title with vigor. They hammered away at me as only graduate students can. We argued its relative merits for a while until one of them, who had been sitting quietly, chimed in with "Nope, that's not the title." I said, "What is the title then?" Jokingly, he said I should entitle it: "See me, hear me, fear me." After laughing out loud, I started to think about how awful his humorous title was. It kind of flows, but I *had* a couple of conductors like that. Didn't you? I remembered hating them. I hated everything they stood for, and I never wanted to be like them.

But then I started thinking. I thought and thought and thought until I finally realized the title of the workshop *should* be changed. The title should really be: "Mizaru, Kikazaru and Iwazaru." Do they ring any bells? Do you remember the three monkeys of Japanese tradition: see no evil, hear no evil, and speak no evil? Thinking about what my student had said made me realize those three monkeys are what we do. That's what it is all about. Three little tiny, invisible monkeys sit on each of our shoulders as we teach. They filter all we say, do and hear. They serve as a musical and pedagogical conscience for us all. With that thought in mind, I really wanted to title the session: "The Three Monkeys On Your Shoulder." I quickly abandoned that idea realizing no one would want to see that!

So those three monkeys are what we are going to discuss in this chapter. Let me introduce you to what we will talk about in relation to those monkeys before we detail each aspect. The first monkey: that *they*, the ensemble, "see no evil." From your hands they see only meaningful communication, nothing confusing. From your face they don't see an expressionless void. Rather, they see an extremely communicative face full of emotions, caring and enjoyment. Remember that *what they see is what you get*. Our students are the most powerful and accurate mirror we as teachers can have. They are merely a reflection of us. As much as that thought can be scary, it is nevertheless true.

The second monkey: neither *you* nor *they* "hear no evil." *They* hear it sounding better, hopefully to the point of sounding good. I know as you read that last line you must be thinking, "I bought this book so some idiot could tell me that I should make it sound better?" But how much rehearsal time is wasted with something not getting noticeably better? It happens all the time. We do something over and over again, but it doesn't necessarily get profoundly better. After a portion of rehearsal that I don't see progress, all I can think is that I just wasted twenty minutes of my students' lives. In addition to hearing it sound better, *they* hear praise and positive reinforcement, that gold-standard of teaching excellence. And lastly, with regard to this monkey, that *you* hear reality. By that I mean critical listening. I don't mean being negatively critical, always seeing the glass as half empty, I mean listening for what really is.

The third monkey: *you* "speak no evil." We must speak effectively so they hear clear, precise, meaningful communication of how to correct errors, how emotions should be portrayed, that we care and that we are enjoying the process as well as the product. I must say that I find some teachers address each of those points by saying to the first one: "I do that every minute of every day." To the second: "Yeah, I'm a pretty emotional guy, I do that a lot." To the third: "They know I care. But am I sure they know I care?" And to the fourth one: "*Enjoy* myself — what the heck are you talking about?" I believe those points are stated above in reverse order of importance. My dad always used to tell me: "I don't care what you do for a living — just make darn sure you enjoy it. Because if you enjoy it — it isn't work." We all know how true that is.

At this point you may be asking yourself why we need to worry about all of this communication. Why are those monkeys so important? I think there are two specific reasons. First, so you get what you truly want, or put otherwise, so your vision for them is realized. You have in your musical heart, soul and mind a preconceived notion of what it is you want them to gain in a rehearsal or from a piece of music. Every one of us walks into our rehearsal with a piece of music playing in our heads. I don't care whether it's grade one or seventeen and a half. We then start rehearsing our fifth-grade band and at that moment we hear reality. In other words, we have the *goal* in our *minds*, and hear the *starting point* in our *ears*. So most importantly, with this communication, we facilitate them coming as close as possible to realizing that goal or vision we have in our heads.

But how many of us bail on our vision? We are all guilty of it at times. As we walk into that rehearsal of *Toccata Marziale* with our high school band, we hear the London Symphony winds playing it in our minds. We stand in front our band. We offer that initial preparation to start the work and we hear this *stuff* coming back at us. We have two options at that moment. We can say "Wow, they ain't never gonna sound like the London Symphony winds," and give up on where we want them to go, or we can tirelessly work to get them there. Will they ever sound that good or get to that goal? Probably not. But we all know that's not what it's all about.

The second reason for all of this communication is to truly engage students in rehearsals. To me that is the key to everything. It is all that really matters. We all know they are not nameless, soulless, faceless entities sitting on chairs in front of us, the artist. They are part of the process, and they have to be engaged in it. If they are engaged in the rehearsal, they will come to its end thinking, "That was enjoyable and seemed to go by so fast." Conversely, if we don't engage them, during every quarter-note rest they will look at the clock in frustration. We all want to engage them, but sometimes it is hard to do. I am often asked how to get them truly involved.

I have two simple rules to help engage students in rehearsals, and I try to live by them. First, give them something meaningful to watch: cues, facial expressions or gestures that mean something to them. Second, give them something meaningful to hear. By that I mean inspire them, give them corrections that truly make things better, and give them enormous amounts of positive reinforcement. If I were told I had to stop using positive reinforcement or end my teaching career, I'd become a chef. I wouldn't stop. I couldn't stop. It is the only tool I've ever learned that really works. To me, educational mumbo-jumbo comes and goes. Positive reinforcement is as true and steady as the sun.

Before we address each of the areas of communication we have just introduced, let me preface them with what I believe are obstacles to communication. They can be obstacles to hearing, such as: fans, heaters, the noise of other classes, or the sound of other ensembles rehearsing. I can't tell you the number of band rooms I've been in where I hear the rumble of a heater fan going full tilt. I often have to wonder is that bass clarinet or heater fan? I remember conducting an all-state band once where we had to rehearse in the gym. As I arrived for my first rehearsal, I was immediately distracted by a piercing, high-pitched buzz coming from the ceiling lights. After several minutes, I realized it would be impossible to work with that non-stop burning of those lights at a slightly flat concert B. It was so loud. I wandered over to the ensemble manager. After telling him that I pride myself on not asking for anything when I go out to conduct, I apologetically asked that we do something about the situation. He very sincerely went to get help.

A few minutes later he returned with a custodian in tow. I beseeched him to get rid of that sound. He said, "No problem, I can do that." Whereby he proudly walked over to the electrical panel and killed the lights. All of them! There we all were in the middle of a great big, windowless gym that was as dark as night. I said, "I don't think that's the solution." He replied, "Well, take your choice, we have two settings: on and off!" We simply had to make due with the situation; thank goodness nothing we were to rehearse was in the key of B major!

Obstacles also take the shape of things that impact our visual communication. Lack of lighting, where kids have to strain to see the page is one such obstacle. As well, often we set up our ensembles so that they are staring directly into sunlight coming through a bank of windows. Often their squinting tells us they are looking right into the surface of the sun. Unless we take the opportunity to occasionally walk over to see their perspective, we might miss that problem. Poles, columns, rails, cabinets and the like offer physical obstacles to sight which we grow accustomed to having in the way. Simple adjustments can make a world of difference. My favorite story about sight obstacles comes from an experience I had conducting in Europe.

I was rehearing an ensemble in a new, all wood, cathedral ceiling band room. The wall against which the conductor stood was all glass. That room was extraordinary. It was nicer than any mountain retreat one could ask for. So I started to rehearse. As I conducted, I watched these players look around in bewildered awe. I stopped to ask for their attention. As I continued, if anything, the problem got worse. I couldn't figure out the dilemma until I turned around and looked out those giant windows. There in front of me was a magnificent, remarkable, startling, overwhelming view of the Alps. The Alps! There stood before us those monuments of nature towering in the sunlight. They were breathtaking. Not wanting to compete with that view, I immediately stopped them, and said, "Gang, guess what we're going to do? We're going to get up and reset the ensemble facing the opposite direction." At that moment, without missing a beat, who else but a trumpet player blurts out: "What, so you get to look at the Alps!"

The reason I bring up these obvious distractions is that we get numb to them. We don't hear or see them anymore. If I were to walk up to you and slap you once across the face it would have great meaning and impact. However, if I continued to slap you, by the thirtieth slap I'm just going to be a nuisance. It's like a smell — we simply get used to it. We can get used to just about anything!

Armed with thoughts of those obstacles, let us detail three types of rehearsal communication. We, the conductor/teacher, can express our wishes with communication from the hands, voice and face. Within each of those types of communication, however, we use various languages.

Communication from the Hands

The first type of communication is from the hands, that nonverbal language of motion and movement. From the hands we need to communicate functional conducting. By that I mean that nonverbal language using a vocabulary of gestures to communicate technical information about a work. That is the passing on of specific data about a work. As stated in an earlier chapter, this is where we can think that the context of one work is different from another, though the content is the same. A sudden accent is a sudden accent. That content is the same. Though certainly the context of that sudden accent will be vastly different between Brahms and Sousa, the vocabulary of gestures remains the same.

From the hands we need also communicate impressionistic conducting. That is the nonverbal language in our hands whereby we communicate the style, emotion, drama and mood of a work. That is the context about which we just spoke.

The next method of communication from the hands is through the use of independence of hands. That is the ability to show two different nonverbal communications, one in each hand, at the same time. When possible and appropriate we should develop our skills to be able to represent two distinctly different rhythms, articulations, dynamics, phrases or the like, at once. In that way we will truly emulate the desired sounds while helping to facilitate those contrasts. I remember a time in a rehearsal at school when the trumpets were having great difficulty with a rhythmic passage. The spot had the ensemble playing in two different meters, executing extremely conflicting rhythms. It was not at all clean. I stopped the group and tried to explain the subtle nuances of the passage. We played it again with little if any improvement. At that moment, in frustration, I stopped them and said, "Is there anything I can do to help?" To which my principal trumpet player, without missing a beat said, "Conduct both meters please." After getting over the fact that I didn't think of that, I did so, and the problem vanished. It never ceases to amaze me how smart our kids are.

The last way we can help communicate from our hands is by developing our own language of quickly recognizable nonverbal signals to represent specific corrections. These need not mean anything to any other conductor. However, by training your ensemble to the specific gestures, they will come to instantly react to the information given, saving great amounts of rehearsal time. For example, putting our left index finger horizontally across our extended tongue could mean that we want them to stop accenting, or our left hand moving horizontally from side to side in an intense manner could mean that we want the sound much more smoothly sustained, even and uninflected. With some creative thinking each of us can find symbols to represent corrections for commonly occurring problems. Though I'm the first one to say that some of those gestures look absolutely goofy, I also know that with them, we can change the articulation of a tuba section that is over-accenting in a split second! No talking, no stopping and restarting, no time spent.

We must remember that all of the above nonverbal communications are predicated on our using them consistently, and teaching our students what each gesture means, like vocabulary words in a foreign language class. As said before, that can best be accomplished during the playing of simple warm-up exercises rather than in the preparation of difficult works. In that way, all of our students' concentration can be on what they see and hear, rather than worrying about technical demands. Their eyes can be focused on our hands and face, and their ears can be focused on the sounds they hear. How crazy is it to try to teach the meaning of a gesture while the ensemble is just trying to stay alive during the playing of a passage of running two hundred fifty-sixth notes! Once gestures are understood in warm-up exercises we can transfer that knowledge and skill to performance music, starting with technically less demanding works and moving slowly to integrate the gestures into more technically demanding compositions.

Before moving on, I must offer a word of warning. Beware — beware — use great care not to mix or replace verbal communication with or for nonverbal communication. If you do, you get a potion I think more poisonous than arsenic. You will end up giving those most awful, distressing, repulsive things we call aural cues. My most hated, vicious and unforgiving enemy. Those communications from the underworld. Quicksand for conductors. The Bermuda Triangle of teachers. The nemesis of nonverbal communication. Whether they be counting off to start an ensemble, tapping the stand, or snapping the pulse, they are all equally debilitating. For if a student can listen for counting off to start him, a tap of the stand to stop him, and the snapping of fingers for everything in between, why on earth would he need to look up at us? He can get everything he needs to minimally play his part without ever seeing if we are in the room! Truthfully, we could probably phone that rehearsal in, rather than be there. Can't you just hear it: "One, two, ready, play...faster, snap, snap, snap...tubas, more legato...clarinets, more accented...ready, phrase...don't rush, snap, snap, snap...stop, tap, tap, tap, tap, tap!" We could do that from the golf course or the living room couch.

The use of verbal or audible sounds to replace nonverbal gestures is usually what we do when we panic. When things aren't working the way we want them to, we often use aural cues as an expedient cure. In the long run, that is like the doctor who after completing surgery states that the operation was a success, but the patient died. Aural cues are the surest way to sabotage any and all nonverbal communication you wish to offer, even if they get "results" at that moment. I usually demonstrate this by asking people to sing two consecutive whole notes at a slow pace. And though I beat a steady tempo while they sing the first time, I tell them in advance that I want a beautiful phrase between the tones. Seeing no nonverbal gesture, the performance is usually absent the phrase. I then repeat the exercise, but this time I yell, "ready phrase" on the beats where they need to execute the phrase. That always gets an improved performance, but is very ragged and nonmusical, with many still not phrasing correctly. The aural cue has helped but not that much. Lastly, I have them repeat the exercise, however this time I say nothing, but I conduct a clear luftpause. That nonverbal gesture always, and I mean always, sounds best: most accurate and most musical. The first performance offered the singers bad conducting technique which got us nowhere. When that failed, I panicked and went to an aural cue: simply replacing lousy technique with verbal directions.

Just because a gesture doesn't work, we can't panic and go to an aural cue. If an initial preparation to start an ensemble doesn't work, we can't resort to counting, "One, two, ready and play now!" We need to fix the gesture. Realize the problem, figure out why the gesture is failing, and get rid of or modify that gesture so as to correct the problem. If they don't stop with you, don't start whacking the stand. That's like training a Skinner mouse or Pavlovian dog. As a player, why would I look up? What would the reason be to expend the extra energy needed to do that?

Every once in a while, I do a portion of a rehearsal without saying a word. I will give rehearsal numbers with my fingers, and try to use my hands and face to communicate everything. No one in the room says a word. A few years ago I was asked to speak at a director's clinic. At that workshop, the three days ended with a rehearsal for all of the directors to observe. After hearing me talk, two of the directors dared me to do a silent rehearsal for half of that session. In that they bet me a cup of coffee, the urgency of the situation grew strong. I upped the ante and said I would do it for the whole rehearsal. They confidently walked away for the lunch break feeling their money was secure. After lunch, I walked onto the podium, showed the ensemble the cover of the score, and started in with my rehearsal. Not a word was spoken. The silence was intense. The energy palpable. After an hour or so, I used that universal time-out symbol to indicate a break. Immediately, those two directors were standing in front of me, begging me to say something — anything — to break the deafening silence. At that moment, wanting to say something profound, I looked them in the eyes and very professorially said: "I drink it black!" Try it, it is more fun than you could imagine!

Communication from the Face

The second type of communication comes from the face. Do you know who teaches the use of communication from the face best? Are you thinking drama, dance, public speaking or drawing? No. Sign language teachers. Why, you may be asking. It is because that language cannot exist without the use of communication from the face. Without facial expressions there can be no sarcasm or inflection. Think about it for a moment. If I say to you, "You are the biggest idiot I have ever known." How would you take that? Surely, if I said it with laughter in my voice and a giant smile on my face, you would know I was being sarcastic. If however, I said it with a scowl on my face, through clenched teeth in the angriest of voices, you would know I meant it in the nastiest way. The true meaning of that statement can only be gotten from inflection and facial expressions. If I were to sign that statement to you, likewise without any facial expression, you would have no way to interpret my sentiment. Several sign language teachers have told me that most deaf people would rather have an interpreter with a highly expressive face, even if his or her hands are a bit sloppy. After learning that, my entire way of viewing the teaching of facial expressions changed. We must truly practice using our face as much as we practice using our hands.

We must non-verbally communicate three different kinds of information with our face. First, can we project the expression and emotion of the music: that indescribable expression of our art? Can we describe feelings like majesty, mournfulness or pouting? Can our face show a reflective, thoughtful look about the music, or portray the awe of a sunrise? To me the face adds a layer of expression to our conducting that words cannot represent. No matter how wonderful our hands are, adding the dimension of facial expression makes it even better. I liken that to an artist who picks the perfect frame for a painting she has finished. That perfect frame will bring out, or make pronounced, every aspect of what the artist wishes to reveal. Is the unframed painting bad? No, but the frame can bring out the best of it and offer the viewer greater depths of understanding. Professor H. Procter-Gregg said it so well when describing the remarkably communicative face of

Sir Thomas Beecham. He said, "Players got what they required mostly from his eyes. As Beecham said: 'There is, you know, a certain current which passes...from the eyes.'"

Second, we must show our enjoyment of our art; that we really, truly love what we are doing. Not that our students *think* we like what we're doing, but that we unquestionably adore it. Third, our face must express our approval or disapproval of their performance at the time. They need to know if what they are doing is what we wanted them to do. They need to know if they are matching our expectations. Undoubtedly, we want them to become self-sufficient, able to self-assess and self-motivate, but we need to help them with that process.

I learned this best from an experience during a concert with my symphonic band at the university. During intermission, one of my bassoonists came up to me back stage, looked me in the eyes, and quite sternly said, "You think it stinks" (she actually used a more ferocious word that I can't repeat here). I said, "Pardon me." She then more vehemently repeated her curt phrase. I responded with a firm denial. We argued back and forth for what seemed to be hours. I said, "It was a wonderful first half and I can't wait to get back for the rest." She then said, "Don't patronize me, I know you think it stinks!" I finally asked her why she thought that. She responded by saying, "Never once in the first half did you go like *this*." As she said the word "this," she threw her head back as if looking to the heavens while fully extending both arms up in the air with hands aimed to the sky as if summoning the forces of nature. Holding back my laughter I said, "You're kidding, right?" She said, "No, I'm really serious; that's how we know you're happy and pleased." I then explained that those compositions simply didn't fit that gesture. As I walked away thinking this was utterly incredible, I saw her look unconvinced of my real thoughts.

Minutes later, the second half of the concert started. Well, I can tell you that in the first piece of the second half I did that gesture no less than three times in places that I'm sure were totally inappropriate. Heck, I'm pretty sure one was even during a grand pause! After the first of those episodes, I looked over to the young lady with my eyes obviously asking if that was better. While still playing her bassoon, she closed her eyes and nodded to the affirmative. She taught me a valuable lesson that evening. Students perceive a lot of things we might not realize they perceive. Whether it's looking to the heavens, a subtle smile, a goofy look, or a grin that only they can see. Rest assured they are looking.

Communication from the Voice

The third type of communication is effective speaking, the verbal languages of words and sounds from our voice. I believe there are eight things we must communicate with our voice. As I think of each of them, I can't help but reflect on the extraordinary words attributed to a great number of people, among them comedian Steve Martin: "Talking about music is like dancing about architecture." What all these ways of communicating with the voice have in common are trying to clearly express our wishes and intent in the quickest possible way. Saving time is, I feel, our primary goal when it comes to verbalizing our desires.

GIVING DIRECTIONS

When giving directions to our students, our instructions must be heard as well as understood. To that end we must speak clearly, making sure that all students can hear us. We must enunciate well and be succinct. We shouldn't wonder why students are tuning us out if we ramble on for twenty words in a soft mumble audible to only the first row. Instead, could our directions have been conveyed precisely with a few well-chosen words? I also think a constantly varying pace of fast and slow, volume of louds and softs, and inflection of highs and lows can keep our students' interest and provide a more enjoyable rehearsal for all.

CORRECTING ERRORS

I am convinced that sometimes people don't stop to correct errors in rehearsals because of how much time they fear it will take to stop, correct the error and then restart the ensemble. We must work on our conducting technique for the stopping and starting, and our effective speaking for the correction of errors. We can't take a "pass" on fixing something due to a lack of confidence in our abilities. To correct errors, we have to be at the "top of our game." We must be ahead of them, anticipating problems before they occur. We all know the key is preparation. For if we are prepared, we are always ready to correct errors, to give praise for something done well, or offer constructive criticism.

A helpful way to engage students and keep them focused while correcting errors is to move them with you as you specify a location in the piece. By saying, "Everyone count with me from letter D, one, two, three, four, five, the sixth measure..." they move through the piece, counting with you and arriving at the spot as you do. Once they get used to this approach they will actually find the spot together, rather than what so often happens. You know, where a third of the group finds the spot immediately and sits waiting, a third of the group doesn't bother to even look for it until you have repeated the location four times, and a third of the group is trying to find it but ends up at different places along the way.

In addition, when correcting errors I believe we need to give them: the *who*, the *where* by location from biggest to smallest marker, *what* is wrong, and then *what* is correct. By saying *who* first, we rid the rehearsal of the problem of giving a location, having everyone find it, and then saying "second bassoons." Didn't that always drive you crazy in rehearsals? You know, when the conductor would say, "Everyone find measure seven hundred thirty-six." You then dutifully started to count. After seemingly hours of counting, you all arrive at the spot only to hear, "Bass drum player, please use a slightly lighter beater, now let's all start at measure twenty-two." After a few of those, no one bothers to find the spot, not even the people who actually are being addressed but don't know it yet. By clearly starting with the who, those *not* involved appreciate not having to find the spot. That avoids them feeling their time is being wasted.

By giving the *where* from big landmark to finest detail of location, we efficiently and systematically get them focused on the problem spot. That deductive manner of funneling their focus seems to work well. For example: "Trumpets, count with me from the trio: one, two, three...twelfth measure, the third beat, the fourth sixteenth note, you are playing an E, it is an E flat." Or, "Everyone, count with me before the end, one...fifteenth measure, last beat, second eighth note, you are playing staccato, it should be molto legato." As you can see, I also like to consistently end with the correction so the last thing they hear "ringing in their ears" is the correct information.

The next three ways we communicate with our voice are musical languages of sounds rather than verbal languages of words. Again, what makes these *languages*, just like the English language of words is consistent use. If one day something is called a "music stand" and the next day it is called a "cat," whatever it is loses any meaning in terms of recognition.

RHYTHM

I advocate using only one language when speaking about or singing rhythms. Though I prefer a version of French time name syllables, I think the consistent use of only one system is more important than which system is used. If during one rehearsal we sing a rhythm as "ti-ti-ti-ti-ta" and during the next it is "one and two and three" and the next it is "scu-bee-du-bee-du," the usefulness of any pedagogical system for rhythm will diminish.

SOUNDING PITCH

Whenever I sing or refer to sounding pitch in rehearsals I use solfeggio. In that way, they will know when I sing in solfege I am referencing the tones as they sound, rather than as they are written. If I sing "do-re-mi-fa-sol" all will know I am singing sounding pitch, even though some will see it as D-E-F#-G-A, while others will see C-D-E-F-G. If I were to sing either of those, others would be left wondering why they don't see those notes on their part.

WRITTEN PITCH

Every time I sing written pitch, I use the letter names applicable to that part, adding the "iese" or "es" suffix to allow for sharps and flats, respectively. In that way, I can sing exactly what the players see with the correct rhythm. For example, if I were to sing "B flat-C-D-E flat-F-G-A-B flat," I would correctly match their letter names and the pitches of a B flat major scale, but would sing a far different rhythm than what the performers see. If they had written quarter notes for every tone, they would wonder why I am singing "eighth-eighth-quarter-quarter-eighth-eighth-quarter-quarter-quarter-eighth-eighth." But by applying the aforementioned system, I can sing "Bes-C-D-Es-F-G-A-Bes," offering the correct pitches as well as rhythm. In that way, chromatic pitches can be sung using one syllable, thus not altering the rhythm of a line in an effort to sing the correct "words" to represent chromatic alterations.

As with sounding pitch and rhythm, the internal consistency of our approach to singing written pitch is key to its usefulness and success. By internal consistency I mean that no aspect of the system contradicts any other aspect of what has been learned in the system. For example, asking an ensemble trained in solfege to sing a major scale using "la" for each tone would be internally inconsistent. They have already been taught that la has a specific meaning within the language they use. In that way, only one of those tones would correctly be called la. For all of the other tones we would, in effect, be asking students to use the word "cat" to refer to what was already labeled as a "music stand."

EMOTIONS, EXPRESSION AND PASSION

I consider this to be the most important thing we need to communicate with our voice. We must develop ways of describing, presenting and talking about this aspect of performance that is meaningful communication. In other words, we need to develop a descriptive language of emotions. I do admit that can be like trying to describe the color yellow to someone who has never had sight. But we must — for if we don't, who will? But *how* do we do it? How do we describe that most elusive gift? The first thing we can do is to prepare ourselves. Though some of us are naturally emotional beings who can cry at the sight of a car battery commercial, others of us have more difficulty expressing our inner self.

For those of you who wish a bit of help, I would suggest reading any of the books of noted speaker and writer Leo Buscaglia. This magnificent gentleman left us a treasure trove of thoughts about expressing emotions. After reading any of his books you will feel differently about what you do and how you do it. I would start with his book *Love*, then *Personhood*. I would suggest savoring every one of his writings. For each offers insight into the joy of sharing our inner person. Those books will undoubtedly start you on your way to being more communicative of your emotions on the podium and in life. We can help our students learn to laugh, cry, find joy, handle sorrow, deal with anger, revel in beauty, and tingle with excitement. What greater gift could we give young people than make them more comfortable with their feelings and learn how to appropriately express them?

We must make certain, however, when speaking about emotion or expression that we use words that have meaning to everyone. I am reminded of the words of Bülow speaking to a trombone player when he said, "Your tone sounds like roast beef gravy running through a sewer." I don't know about you, but I have no idea what that actually means, and I am positive that if this were expressed to me, I would have no idea what to do. I remember watching a rehearsal once with a friend. During the rehearsal, the conductor stopped the group with a yell and shouted, "No, I want that yellow rose sound!" The players sat there in front of him looking around with puzzled expressions, wondering if anyone understood. They started playing again, only to be stopped almost instantly with the shouting of "No, a *yellow* rose sound!" Finally, my friend leaned over to me and asked what that meant. To which I replied I had no idea, and that I was hoping he knew. They started again, and this time the shouting of "yellow rose" was angrier. At that point my friend leaned over to me and whispered, "They must be doing that *red* rose sound." I thought after that, the *third* time, there would surely be an explanation. No explanation. He finally looked at them with glaring eyes and heatedly said, "You are just not capable of a yellow rose sound," and ordered them to move on to the next composition. To this day I have no idea what the heck a yellow rose sound was supposed to be. It obviously meant something very powerful to him; we just have to make sure it means something to our students.

Now I am not saying we can't use lots of wonderful anecdotes, metaphors and descriptive phrases. We just have to make certain they are useful and truly communicative. I recall a rehearsal at a festival where we were working on a composition that portrayed the moon in all its grand steadiness while the evening stars twinkled in the background. My interpretation viewed them as two distinct entities. During the rehearsal, I described how I wanted each to be performed to capture that image. The stars were to be little bursts of light in a short, percussive and soft manner with great amounts of decay, while the moon lingered with sustained dank wallowing sounds. A bit later in the rehearsal, just as one of the host teachers walked in, I stopped the ensemble and blurted out, "No, there are just too many stars and not enough moon!" The look on that teacher's face was priceless. I am not sure who he thought was crazier: me for saying it, or the players for understanding what I meant? Sometimes that kind of descriptive context is so very necessary, and is the only way to communicate our interpretation. I could have described what I wanted in purely technical, mechanical terms, but it would have been lifeless, void of passion and probably much more time consuming.

THAT WE CARE

We must communicate that we care with our words, face and manner. We have to show our students we truly care about *them*. As the old phrase reminds us, "They won't care how much you know until they know how much you care." Those profound words are so true. If they feel that we are in it for them because we really, passionately care about them as human beings and musicians, and about the art of music, they will forgive anything. How we accomplish *that* is a very personal thing. Each of us does it in our own way.

In an effort to express that, I never refer to players by their names in rehearsals, only by their instruments. Even those I have known for years. They are always referred to as "timpani" or "first trumpet." Though this may seem like I am so uncaring as to not bother to learn names, I tell them I intentionally do that to constantly reinforce that no matter how disappointed or distressed I am at that instrumental part, I am never disappointed or distressed at the person playing the part. It is not just semantics. I want them to know that I view each of them at all times as wonderfully remarkable human beings. As well, when walking on stage for any performance, I have always, and I mean always, bowed to the ensemble first, then the audience. I do that as an expression of my respect for the players and as a sign of my appreciation for all they have done. I want them to know that *they* are truly the most important part of the performance; not me and not the audience. Lastly, I always try to admit when I make a mistake. I do that to show them I am as critical of my performance as I have been of theirs, and that I am constantly trying to improve.

OUR EXPECTATIONS

The last thing we must convey with our voice is our expectations. I believe that our expectations are the filter through which everything we do must pass. Our expectations are the guide, stimulus and catalyst for studying scores, planning rehearsals, pacing rehearsals, motivating, disciplining, and developing short and long-range goals and objectives for an ensemble. In trying to come up with a cogent explanation of my philosophy regarding a conductor's expectations for an ensemble, I arrived at what I call *The Expectation Spiral*. It is my hope that this analogy will better explain my feelings on the topic. Philosophies and approaches to conducting are as numerous as the people who conduct. Perhaps no other facet of our art yields more opinions or passionate beliefs than what our expectations should be.

The extremes run from the school of thought that advocates a conductor using anger and intimidation to engender fear in their players, to those who agree with the admonition that states that players are responsible for everything. That second approach maintains that players must take it upon themselves to learn the music, define goals, develop self-discipline, and work as an ensemble to identify problems and correct them. The former approach is loathsome. The latter, I believe, is giving up too much responsibility for our job. Though self-guidance is enviable in many ways, that philosophy often does little but allow a group to stew in its own inability or ability as the case may be. I hope the following describes my approach, which I think is somewhere in the middle of those two extremes.

The Expectation Spiral. One of the great joys in my life was learning to fly an airplane. Strangely, I tend to view and relate so much in my life to flying, especially teaching and conducting. I am convinced that the same abilities, attitudes, zeal, joie de vivre, dexterity, perception, coordination, courage, and refined motor skills that make for a fine pilot make for a fine conductor. As pilots and teachers we must possess: the ability to be calm in a storm, act rather than react, assess circumstances with speed and precision, constantly monitor surroundings, and respond to a situation with the correct technique though it may go contrary to what seems logical. As well, we must control a powerful entity capable on the one hand of causing unbelievable disaster, and on the other hand of creating feelings of awesome beauty. In classes and rehearsals I relate many sounds, images and effects to flying.

One of my favorite analogies between flying and teaching corresponds to our expectations. We constantly have to wrestle with how hard to push an ensemble. What is an appropriate goal, and when should it be reached? When should we back-off, when should we settle, when should we praise and when should we criticize? Those questions all relate to two factors: the final goal and how we get there.

If we achieve the goal, but the ensemble hates us and the experience, that is obviously catastrophic. If we achieve the goal, but the ensemble hates the music, that is failure. We must find a way to press players to achieve the best they can, as fast as they possibly can, while respecting them as people. A conductor who achieves goals while destroying the emotional well-being of a player is repulsive. Conversely, conductors who are so concerned with being liked that they allow a free-for-all atmosphere have given-up responsibility to their students and their art.

I believe we must all be ourselves, and be the conductor that best matches our disposition and personality. I do not advocate being fake on the podium. I think we must all find our own best way of producing our goals with insight, vigor and efficiency. We should never settle for less than we think an ensemble is capable of, however, we should never demand more from an ensemble than they are able to achieve. Fear, hatred, screaming and cursing are motivational. But to what end? Do they serve the musicians or the music? Do they embody the joy, power and beauty of music? Do they cause performers to respond to the conductor with feelings of respect, admiration, trust and the knowledge that the conductor is in this for the right reasons? Do they empower the players with a sense of pride, faith in their abilities, willingness to try, and a love of music and art? Most importantly, do students get a message that to play better, they need to try harder, even if that means exposing themselves to the risk of failing? In other words, do they know they can try so hard that they may indeed fail?

How, you ask, does this have anything to do with flying? Well, let me describe a scene. Picture flying along at eight thousand feet in the air. As you sit there with the wind soaring past you, the motor noisily running and the propeller forcefully cutting through the air, you hear the unmistakable sound of the engine quitting. That sound of "fltfltfltfltfltfltfltflt...fltfltfltfltflt...fltfltflt...fltflt...flt!" You immediately go through the procedures to restart the engine. They all fail. You are now at eight thousand feet in the air and about to land, one way or another. As you were going through your steps to restart the engine, you were also checking your surroundings for a landing site. All along, as a fine pilot you were keeping abreast of your position and noting possible landing sites in the event of an emergency. You recall that directly under you is a small airport. What luck. You have a place to land.

In that situation you have a very specific goal: to get to the end of that small runway in an approach that will enable you to land. Unfortunately, how you get there is equally important. Without an engine, you will only get one shot at that landing. It must be perfect the first time. You can waste no time. You have a set amount of time to get to that goal. There is no time to waste on anything that doesn't aid your situation. You must use all of your abilities and the plane's capabilities at peak efficiency. Funny, that sounds as much like conducting as it does like flying.

Our desire as a conductor is to achieve the goal of having an ensemble perform a work the best it possibly can at a pre-prescribed time in the future. We will have a small, finite period of time to reach that goal. Thus, we can waste no time or do anything that will not aid in reaching that goal. We will only get one shot at the rehearsal time we have before that performance, so we must be at our best. As you can see, I believe those two situations to be the same. The analogy to flying I am describing is that of a spiral versus a spin.

Every pilot must learn to get out of the above situation by using what is called a spiral. From your starting position up in the air you execute and maintain a very steep turn as you descend. As you continue this downward spiraling motion, you adjust the steepness of the spiral to allow you to come out of the turn at the appropriate time and position to land safely. You must press the airplane's capabilities and your skills to achieve that goal with certainty and precision. You cannot become flustered, frustrated or frightened, or shy away from the severity of your effort. You may have to demand more from yourself and your craft than you ever have, but you must do so with constant control. You can never lose sight of the goal or allow the plane to move off course. Done well, at any moment when the ground appears and you are at landing altitude, you can pull out of the turn and guide your plane to the runway. It always works.

If, however, you allow the turn to become less steep, venturing away from the spiral, no matter what your intentions, you will fail to reach the goal. You will make each turn so wide, albeit comfortable, that you will end up getting to ground level so far away from the field as to never reach your goal. You will happily enjoy the comfortable ride, but probably end up landing in someone's petunia patch.

The opposite problem, I believe, is even more disastrous. If you make the turn too steep and incorrectly demand more than the aircraft is capable of, you may enter what is called a spin. This often-uncontrollable path has the aircraft going straight down with the wings moving in a spinning motion. It is the sight often shown in war movies. You do end up getting to that airport, however you crash in a big ball of flames. By pressing too hard to reach the goal, we will fail. Spins are sometimes retrievable. Fine pilots can recognize them early and take corrective action. Sadly though, if left in a spin too long, some aircraft cannot survive the strain of pulling out of one. The wings will simply come off.

If we as conductors lose sight of our goals, and continually allow rehearsals to go on tangents, we will never reach these goals. That is where we talk too much and rehearse too little, or rehearse without a clear purpose. That is where fun reigns over progress and growth. That is the quintessential example of not having any idea where you're going, but having a lot of fun getting there. Conversely, if we apply too much pressure, pull the reins in too tight, demand more than the ensemble is capable of, or progress faster than they can master, we will end up reaching our goal with a disastrous outcome. This is when players end up hating the conductor, their peers and worst of all, the music. That is when players quit on a regular basis. That is when the end does not justify the means.

Rather, we must fly a perfect spiral. In that way, we will never be so far away that we don't make it to our goal, or fly so violently we put ourselves into a spin. We must constantly encourage, positively reinforce, press for and require progress, growth, hard work, achievement and concentration. We must never allow the focus of our work to venture away from our goals. We must apply firm but appropriate pressure toward that goal. As Frank Battisti so succinctly stated, it is "...never accepting today what was acceptable yesterday."

However, we must never push players harder than what is possible, or beyond their capabilities. We must never allow a person to reach the goal through verbal or mental abuse. We must earn each player's respect, appreciate it, guard it and be ever mindful of it. We must respect every individual, and never allow him or her to lose sight of the ultimate goal: through excellence, gain the ability to communicate, appreciate, enjoy and love music. I believe a great musical experience is the best way to sell a person on continued hard work and motivate him or her to progress.

Please don't think I am saying that straying from a goal is never fruitful. There are always moments in a rehearsal for which no one could plan. Lighthearted moments, stories, almost meditative silence, and work on related techniques and skills are wonderful, useful and beneficial. When I refer to reaching a goal, that goal is far greater than playing the dots on a page. It includes ensemble playing skills such as balance, blend and intonation. It also includes knowledge of the history, theory and science of music as well as related subjects. All of those aspects of being a fine musician are part of our goal. The last thing I would want anyone to think is that I am advocating insensitively and repeatedly pounding technical passages into an ensemble at every rehearsal. Conversely, I believe the successful conductor makes certain that everything done in a rehearsal serves the ultimate goal. Whether it is a story to relax and calm heightened tensions, an exercise to facilitate the learning of a technical passage, or the viewing of a photo to better explain the style of a work, those are all wonderful means to a goal.

As well, we must all realize that some days will be better than others. Some days we progress more than we thought possible, and others we can't even get the ensemble to get out of its own way. We must learn when we can press, and when we should back-off. Settling for less than we wanted today, but keeping control through a positive rehearsal will allow us to succeed on another day. Conversely, if we do not realize that, we will press our students beyond what is possible, and risk the consequences. That is the quintessential example of winning the battle, but losing the war.

By way of example, I tell a story of rehearsing an ensemble when I was a university teaching assistant working on my master's degree. In one of my first rehearsals of the university band, I began working on the opening of Verdi's Overture to *Nabucco*. After explaining to the low brass how I wanted the passage to be performed, I had them play it over and over again. After each playing, I further explained what I wanted. That cycle continued for what seemed like a lifetime. As I began to get more and more frustrated, and they began to get more and more angry, the cycle became a vicious, and I mean vicious, cycle. Not only did the performance cease to get better, it got worse. In a panic, I stopped and told them to take a break. During the break, my mentor came onto the stage, walked up to me, put his arm on my shoulder, leaned over and whispered, "I bet you'll never do that again." Those calm, dispassionate words were said by someone who knew I had to learn that difficult lesson the hard way. He was right. I always remember that day and whenever I start to press an ensemble what I think may be too hard, I think carefully before venturing too far down that road again.

There will be times when we will have to accept less than what we want. It may be due to anticipation the day before a vacation, the excitement of a snowfall, the gloom of a rainy day, the pressures of exam week, or something as awful as the death of a student or teacher. I am not saying we should give up, or allow chaos, but we must press with care, and settle for slightly less. Never stepping over the line, we will always have tomorrow. If, however, we resort to anger and fear, the cost may be too great. We can't ever let the ensemble bring us down. We can't let them lower our expectations. We must remain in control at all times. We simply must accept the fact that some days will be more productive than others. I try to remember the words Bernard Shore used to describe the expectations of Arturo Toscanini. He said

Toscanini "...is never satisfied, but he seems to have an exact picture of the utmost any orchestra can achieve."

We all have high expectations. We demand a lot from our ensembles. I think that is good as long as what we are asking for is appropriate and they possess the readiness to achieve what we seek. Are they emotionally, physically and mentally ready for what we expect? If so, we can work toward great achievements. Are our expectations age appropriate? Just because a group is young doesn't mean it can't achieve a great deal; we will simply have to work in smaller steps. I guess it all boils down to being sensitive to the ensemble. Sensing when enough is too much, and when too much isn't enough.

Years ago I was asked by my Dean to have a pops concert with the band. Though I have nothing against that idea, I didn't want to replace one regular concert with a pops concert. So I decided to propose to the players that we would not replace the concert, but add it. We would not disrupt our concert schedule but instead take one day for the pops concert. We would sight-read the music at 2:30 p.m. and perform it at 7:00 o'clock that night. And just to raise the ante I chose one work to be completely sung as a choir. I thought this would really force us to rehearse with intensity. They all loved the idea, or so they thought. On the afternoon of the concert, our goal was looming pretty brightly. Well, needless to say, the rehearsal was vibrant. The students were wonderful — they never worked harder. The motivation of knowing fifteen hundred people would be arriving to hear them in a few hours probably had something to do with that.

After the rehearsal, we all ran to get changed into concert dress. I quickly changed into my tuxedo. Possibly too quickly. The hour arrived. The group took the stage. I walked out to the podium. As I was getting ready to start the first piece, I saw and heard the start of giggling. The giggles turned to laughter, the laughter to guffaws. In my hurry I seemed to have forgotten that cardinal rule of checking my zipper. Yes, it was down. As I realized my problem, the students were beside themselves. Well, I can tell you from experience there is no graceful way of pulling one's zipper up in front of an ensemble and fifteen hundred audience members. I can still hear the "zzzzzz" sound it made booming through the hall. The echo had to have lasted for hours! We all found it pretty darn amusing. I was laughing so hard that tears were coming down my face. The students weren't laughing at my zipper. They found a perfect way to release tension. They cured themselves. Would I ever schedule it that way again? Sure, but only if I remembered to *forget* to zip my trousers. They showed me when they needed a break from the tension.

So the next time we think about our goals and how to reach them, we need to decide whether our course will be a spiral made through planning, preparation, knowledge, patience, hard work, vigilance, respect, gentleness, calm and love. Or will it be a spin induced by anger, frustration, lack of knowledge, poor planning, or the inability to respond to the psyche of the ensemble. The spiral I believe is the only way. It's severe at times, it's not always the most comfortable way, but it's a pleasant ride down and you'll always get to your goal safely. To me, it is a simple choice. I will leave the final word on this topic to the great Michelangelo, who said, "The greater danger for most of us is not that our aim is too high and we miss it, but that it is too low and we reach it." It is truly a balancing act.

Critical Listening

As important as effective speaking is, I always try to remember that the *best* talkers are also great *listeners*. That brings us to the next topic. Equally important to offering good communication is good listening, or what I call critical listening. The first step is that we should listen rather than read. If we are reading the score, we really can't be effectively listening. Secondly, we need to hear the truth, hear reality rather than what we want to hear. It is all well and good to have an image of what we want, but we must hear what it really sounds like so we can move from there.

Next, we should listen for what I call consonant mistakes. They are errors that don't sound bad or ugly but are errors nonetheless. They are rarely obvious, glaring or offensive. They usually sound very nice, so we don't suspect an error as much. We usually don't hear mistakes that sound *pretty* as easily or critically as those that sound like fingernails on a blackboard. Consonant mistakes are easy to miss. We are lulled by their attractive, albeit incorrect sound. They usually take shape as everyone executing something "together" but inaccurately, such as everyone playing what sounds like a dotted half note followed by a quarter rest when they all have a whole note. Or they may be found as wrong playing that sounds like it fits in, such as the playing of incorrect octaves. I always think it's a shame that all errors can't sound like a minor second being played when it should be a perfect unison!

We also need to listen for conceptual problems as opposed to mistakes. Is it that they don't understand a concept or was it simply a boo-boo? If it is a mistake, that is really almost insignificant. If it is a conceptual problem or error in their understanding of a concept, we need address that deficiency in their understanding if we really want to correct the problem. When it comes to listening with a critical ear, we must constantly be aware of problems, but listen to the big picture as well as the minutia of details.

Conclusion

I believe that if we listen critically, engage our students in rehearsals, give them something meaningful to watch and hear, and show them our caring, expectations, emotions and enjoyment, we will do more than effectively communicate in rehearsals. We will help them dig way down and touch their very souls. To do that, it never ceases to amaze me that a student must process five communications simultaneously: the graphic languages of notation (rhythm, concert pitch and written pitch), the nonverbal languages of the conductor, the verbal languages of the conductor's speech, and the written languages of words on a printed page (instructions, text and terms), all the while expressing themselves emotionally in ways that are intangible.

For our part, I think it all boils down to a quality very hard to describe. As Harold Schonberg asserted, a conductor must above all have that "…mysterious thing known as projection: the ability to beam his physical and musical personality directly forward into the orchestra…." Through that communication we can rehearse effectively and allow our students to grow. We can *teach*. Adapting that old familiar poem, we can remember that "A teacher is one who knows who you are, understands where you have been, accepts who you have become and still gently invites you to grow." In the words of William A. Ward, "The mediocre teacher tells. The good teacher explains. The superior teacher demonstrates. The great teacher inspires." ▰

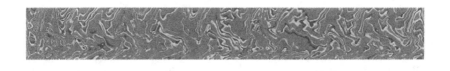

Plain Vanilla Conducting

Picture it. A nice big dish of plain vanilla ice cream. Do you like vanilla ice cream? What if I told you that you would be eating four scoops of that dairy confection at every meal for a year? Do you think you would still like plain vanilla ice cream at the end of that time? Or by then would the very thought of a vanilla bean make you gag? Now don't get me wrong, I like vanilla ice cream. No, I actually love good old plain vanilla ice cream. But let me ask you a question: no matter how much you like vanilla ice cream, after a few months of that regimen wouldn't you like to have a scoop or two of mocha-peanut-cherry-fudge-swirl-caramel-delight? Or at the very least come across a chocolate covered almond in one of those scoops of plain vanilla?

Are we serving the conducting equivalent of plain vanilla ice cream to our students every measure of every work, every day of every month? I'm not talking about correct conducting versus incorrect conducting. The analogy to that would be asking if you wanted to eat spoiled or rotten vanilla ice cream. You would find even one spoonful of that unacceptable. I'm talking about the simply redundant motions of everything conducted the same way. That sameness of conducting, no matter how correct, is debilitating in its repetitiveness. A nice slice of plain white bread is wonderful with its mellow, soft, bland and familiar taste and texture. But sometimes don't you just want to bite into a chewy, coarse-textured, fourteen-grain brown bread? I know I do. And I believe our students do as well.

I like to relate this idea to the English lessons and classes we have had throughout our schooling. In second grade, we were taught vocabulary words. Let's say we just learned the word "cat." We would have to read the word "cat" ninety times, write the word "cat" twenty times, then write ten sentences each using the word "cat" three times. Over and over we would use the word "cat" until we knew it cold. Now fast forward in time to eleventh grade. Do you remember writing essays for English class and getting points off for using the same word twice in one essay? Heck, forget about the days of making certain to use that word three times in one sentence, it was considered reprehensible to use a word twice in one paragraph! Points, however, were given if you used the word "cat," then "feline," "kitty," "tabby" or "the-animal-that-is-petrified-of-dogs." Likewise, when we learned those conducting patterns and gestures, we practiced them over and over and over until we knew them cold. Now we must constantly strive to add variety, to rid our movements from the sameness of our, albeit correct, conducting.

Sometimes it isn't that we don't try to add variety to our conducting; it's that what we do is "half-baked." I remember once being served a beautiful-looking plate of roast chicken at an extremely fine restaurant. It was crispy looking, almost caramel colored in appearance with generous amounts of spice readily apparent. My mouth watered as I looked upon it in anticipation of its taste. I lifted my knife and fork, readied my taste buds, and cut into it for my first bite. As I looked down at my plate, I saw to my horror and sadness that it was raw inside. It was truly half-baked. Any recipe, no matter how great, no matter how perfectly the ingredients are assembled, if not cooked well enough won't be edible, let alone taste like that great recipe should.

For us as conductors, this translates to the fact that no matter how good our score study has been or how great our interpretation is, if our gestures are half-baked, in other words not clear, obvious and confidently executed, our desired result probably won't happen. If you don't courageously show your interpretive wishes, the ensemble probably won't do them. The solution I believe is that we must be creative in our interpretation so we may bring variety, nuance and contrast to our conducting. We must also be *evangelical* in our portrayal of what we want, willing to boldly take a chance even if we trip and fall. We must be impassioned in the projection of our musical desires. Our hands, face and body must implore our performers to do what we ask, what the *music* demands.

I wrote the preceding paragraph as I was flying high above the Rocky Mountains of Colorado. As I looked out the window and stared at their majesty, intensity and contrasts, all I could think was that they are truly *evangelical* mountains. There's no two ways about it. They are clearly, boldly and unquestionably mountains. Obvious in their design, profound in their vividness, and infinite in their variety. I can't imagine anyone looking at them and wondering if what they were seeing were mountains. But just because they are obvious doesn't mean they aren't replete with subtle nuances and tiny details. That's the way our communication can be.

Please don't think for a second what I'm advocating is the constant use of grotesque, enormous, over-conducted gestures. On the contrary, I'm suggesting clear, specific, well-honed movements to achieve contrasts and subtleties of extreme soft, delicate and tender as well as equally extreme power, vibrancy and might. We need to master those two extremes as well as every step between them. We can achieve that goal through what I call the *Empowerment Cycle*. If we have developed our conducting skills to be able to communicate impressionistically as well as functionally with a vocabulary of meaningful gestures, it will free us from worry or concentration about the mechanics of how our hands are used. If we have intensely studied the score, so we have it truly learned, and have developed an interpretation that attends to the variety of details in the work, our minds will be free from concern over knowing when and what is happening at any given time in the work. Then we can boldly use fully-baked, confident, communicative gestures that foster the variety of details in the work. That will empower you to elicit from the ensemble the vision of the composition you have in your heart, mind and soul.

Armed with how we can work to empower our ability to communicate, let's discuss *what* we can communicate to try to avoid the sameness of conducting described above. We can look for shades of difference, lack of contrasts, subtle nuances, coalesced melding, intentional monotony or extreme contrasts of articulation, dynamics, phrase lengths, tone color and style. In addition, the micro-styles and less than obvious buried treasures of "blue corn" that were discussed in reference to score study have to be represented and emphasized in our conducting. We can portray key tones or stress points and moments of tension and repose, always representing the shape, contour and direction of a line. As well, to prevent the unintentional sound of wandering aimlessly, we must be ever mindful of the goal orientation of each section of a composition.

Think about where on your sonic canvas you will "paint" each sound. Does the music need to sound choppy and pointed with a great deal of metric weight on downbeats, or more sustained with evenly weighted pulses? To emulate those sounds we would want more vertical movement with less rebound for the former and more horizontal movement with exaggeratedly stretched rebounds for the latter.

Are the sounds predominantly light, delicate or high in tessitura warranting a higher placement of motion to match the sounds? Or are they heavy or low in tessitura suggesting motion at the bottom of our canvas? Do we show where on our sonic canvas entering imitative lines appear? Are layers of sound represented visually? Can we show contrasts of pompous and demure, weak and strong, whimsical and pensive, elation and sorrow, nasty and warmhearted, elegant and haggard, refined and course, tumultuous and calm, majestic and sinister, or mechanical and spinning freely?

In addition to simply offering the requisite cues with sameness of manner, style, gesture and location on our canvas, can we aim our cues more specifically and exaggeratedly? Can we place cues where the players *are* around the ensemble and with gestures more evocative of the sounds we want? When a passage is homorhythmic in nature do we attend to that in our conducting or do we simply beat time? Do we appropriately use the independence of hands we have developed to show two different styles, rhythms, dynamics, tessituras, events or articulations when occurring in the work? Do we appropriately use either the takt or rebound of our beat motion to act as a catalyst for rhythmic motion?

In short, do we non-verbally offer as much of a description of the composition as possible in our hands? Do our students see sameness or a true portrayal of every aspect of the work? Do we always ask them to eat that plain vanilla ice cream or is our conducting more like a bowl of Rocky Road? Or should I have picked a flavor with a more positive adjective in it? How about butter pecan? Try some. I hope you'll agree that vanilla ice cream is delicious on occasion, but the joys of a bowl of butter pecan are amazing.

"What's Hiding in an Empty Box?"
or
Is Passion
a Four-Letter Word?

I once got a fortune cookie that simply read: "What's hiding in an empty box?" What a remarkable question. Think about it! What is hiding in an empty box? Is it a void? A great big nothingness? Is the box then worthless? Does this question ring negatively to you? It's bad, right? Or does it represent limitless potential? A wonderful open space waiting to be filled? Surely if something is *hiding*, that box *isn't* empty. We just haven't found what's in it. I sometimes think this can be a metaphor for the emotion, passion and expressiveness of our students. Not to imply that they are empty, but that though they may not show much emotion, they have limitless potential! We have to help them find what's hiding within them. We have to help fill them with the joy of music, human emotions, hard work, creativity and curiosity. We have to share our expressiveness and emotions to help them to do the same. Just because we can't see it, doesn't mean it's not there. We just have to help it appear. Let's face it, when it comes to expressing emotions sometimes our students can be, to borrow words from Winston Churchill, "A riddle wrapped in a mystery inside an enigma."

Of all the responsibilities we have as music teachers I believe the preceding paragraph describes what must be our ultimate goal. We have to help students express, understand, deal with, share and find joy in their emotions, all of their emotions. Quite frankly, missing an accidental or playing an incorrect articulation is meaningless in the life of a child. Learning to express themselves freely can invigorate the lives of our students. To me that is all that matters. It is the reason we teach. It is the reason we conduct. It is the reason we are musicians. Music without expression is void of its humanity, its connection to our hearts and souls. It is meaningless. We possess the power to be expressive, to show the magnitude of every human emotion. We also possess the ability to "go through the motions" in a lifeless, dry, routine and unemotional way.

In his book on the great maestro Pablo Casals, David Blum describes how "Casals hated that which was sterile, cold and lifeless. A 'correct' performance held no interest for him if it failed to communicate the essential glory of music, its ability, through the beauty of its contours, the depth and range of its expression, to move us to the heart. When confronted with a student unwilling to make an interpretive commitment, Casals would say: 'It is even better to do something in bad taste than to be monotonous.'" Casals went on to say, "Don't give notes — give the meaning of the notes!" Or as the remarkable composer Gustav Mahler stated, "What is best in music is not to be found in the notes." The profound words of Sidney Lanier express this so eloquently: "Music is love in search of a word."

A few years ago I heard a wonderful description of emotions in music. One afternoon I was sitting in my office when the telephone rang. Answering the phone, I heard a voice say, "I have to read you something." Not "hello" or "how are you" or even who was speaking. I came to realize it was a graduate student of mine. She very excitedly went on to tell me that she had to read me a quote from a paper written by one of her high school students. Over the telephone she recited a quote her student had found. Though the author was unknown, the words nonetheless expressed what music meant to her: "Music is what feelings sound like." She got it. Somewhere along the line she came to understand what was truly important in music. I don't know who was more excited: that student, her teacher, or that teacher's teacher!

The power of what we do as music teachers is truly remarkable. It never ceases to amaze me. No matter how many times I see young people share their emotions I am filled with a sense of purpose and awe. I treasure the memories of those times. I will, however, never forget one such occasion. It was after the performance of a weekend honors band festival. After talking with people backstage, I wandered back to the podium on that empty stage to gather my belongings. Or so I thought the stage was empty. As I packed my briefcase I looked back to see one young boy still sitting in his chair in the middle of the trumpet section. He was crying. I walked back and quietly sat down next to him. After a few moments, through the tears he told me his grandfather had died several months ago, and that this was the first time he was able to cry. We sat on that stage for quite some time. Though few words were spoken, volumes were expressed.

For as long as I live I will believe that we as music teachers do this better than anyone. To me it's like that wonderful character Tigger, from *Winnie the Pooh*. As he bounced around the Hundred Acre Wood boldly saying, "Bouncin', why that's what Tiggers do best!" Passion, emotions, and expression: that's what we do best. I have often recalled the words of an experienced English teacher quoted by William Mitchell in his book *The Power of Positive Students*. Addressing that which was truly important in a young person's education, the anonymous teacher wrote, "I have taught young people for ten years. During that time I have given assignments, among others, to a murderer, an evangelist, a boxer, and a thief. The murderer was a quiet little boy who sat in the front seat and regarded me with pale blue eyes; the evangelist, easily the most popular boy in school, had the lead in the junior play; the boxer lounged by the window and let loose at intervals a raucous laugh that startled the geraniums; the thief was a lighthearted Lothario with a song on his lips. The murderer awaits death in the state penitentiary; the evangelist has lain a year now in the cemetery; the boxer lost an eye in a brawl in Hong Kong; and the thief, by standing on tiptoe, can see the windows of my classroom from the county jail. All these pupils once sat in my room, sat and looked at me across worn brown desks. I must have been a great help to these pupils — for I taught them the rhyming scheme of the Elizabethan sonnet and how to diagram a complex sentence." Every time I read those words I become more convinced of our true mission.

That mission can be summed up best with a story written by Ellen Kreidman about the remarkable author and lecturer Leo Buscaglia. She states that he "once talked about a contest he was asked to judge. The purpose of the contest was to find the most caring child. The winner was a four-year-old child whose next-door neighbor was an elderly gentleman who had recently lost his wife. Upon seeing the man cry, the little boy went into the old gentleman's yard, climbed onto his lap and just sat there. When his mother asked him what he had said to the neighbor, the little boy said, 'Nothing, I just helped him cry.'" We as music teachers just have to help them cry. Because if we don't, quite possibly no one else will.

We have to be willing to show our emotions and passion about music. They need to see that it's okay to feel those emotions as well as share their emotions with us, and with their world. We have to find ways to meaningfully describe and talk about the emotional content of music, whether they are feelings of anger or love, aggression or solace, joy or sorrow. In our controlled environment students can come to work through all these emotions. I have no compunctions about laughing out loud in rehearsals, or crying out loud in concerts. Getting a little crazy in a rehearsal, having students think you're a bit insane, is truly liberating. For some, that thought is frightening, even embarrassing. To that I say, borrowing a sentiment from Dr. Martin Luther King, Jr., if fear of looking silly knocked on the door, and faith in the joy of music answered, there would be no one there.

This comes down to one being willing to emote unconditionally. Our expressiveness cannot be predicated on them giving back or reciprocating the emotion. We must be resolved to move forward even if we fear our students will make fun of us. We must keep in mind that often we make fun and joke about those things that make us uncomfortable, even though that may be something we are extremely concerned about. As George Bernard Shaw said, "When a thing is funny, search it carefully for the truth." We must convince students that no matter how scary it is to put their hearts out there for all to see, open to ridicule as well as to being comforted, it is far healthier than keeping their emotions bottled up inside them.

We must be the generator or catalyst for their expression. We must be the spark. Certainly we want our students to be able to express emotion without us. But until they gain experience doing so, we may have to help them along. We have to connect with them, and help them to connect with us and their musical world. We have to help them find the beauty in all that surrounds them. We must be evangelical in our efforts to promote and project expression. As Sir Thomas Beecham so eloquently declared, "Thought and feeling — notably feeling — are all that matter. Say what you want to say, with firmness and conviction. The one thing that is really important, in playing, in conducting — yes, and even in misconducting — is this: whatever you do, do it with conviction."

To illustrate this better, let me try to describe an episode from the television series M*A*S*H. Those weekly stories told of the trials, accomplishments and sorrows of the men and women assigned to a U. S. Army field hospital during the Korean War. At the start of this episode, Father John Francis Patrick Mulcahy, the camp chaplain, was told he was to be visited by the Divisional Chaplain, Col. Maurice Hollister. He was coming to observe Mulcahy in action. That Sunday morning, Father Mulcahy offered his usual calm and mild-mannered camp worship service. After it was over, the good Father stood quietly at the lectern gathering his belongings. Colonel Hollister, who had been seated among the congregation observing, walked toward Father Mulcahy and stood silently watching with a look of disapproval, concern and consternation. After a few awkward moments, Father Mulcahy sheepishly half looked up at the Colonel and said, "Well sir, seemed to go rather smoothly, didn't it?" With a subdued and sullen voice Colonel Hollister replied, "So does wallpaper paste, Father. You never once had them in the palm of your hand." With a bit more anxious sound in his voice, the Colonel continued by saying, "You've got to grab these people. You're God's messenger in this camp."

In an effort to appease his observer, Father Mulcahy quietly and plaintively rationalized his performance by stating, "Sir, I deliver a...." But before he could finish the thought Colonel Hollister loudly interrupted him and agitatedly retorted, "Many a business has gone bankrupt with the motto we deliver." Now with an even louder voice and an ever-accelerating pace, he heatedly went on to say, "You've got to take these people by the hand, Father. You've just got to reach out and take them by the hand. Each and every one, from the lowliest private here right up there to Capt. Harry S. Truman. You've got to guide them. You've got to lead them. Oh yes, oh yes, you've got to be the one. You've got to be the drum major that leads this band right into the valley of blessedness." With fire brimming in his eyes, a voice as big as thunder and a personality full of rage and power he continued by saying, "You have to use that voice of yours Father, as a cry into the wilderness. Follow me, you see, follow me." As Father Mulcahy looked on in awe, Colonel Hollister now with a thrillingly full and resonant voice, dogmatic inflection and arms and hands extended to the heavens proclaimed, "Lead the attack Father, with a Bible in one hand and a sword in the other!" After witnessing this outpouring of emotion, this display of evangelical zeal, Father Mulcahy looking mesmerized, spellbound and enraptured gazed at his mentor and shouted, "Hallelujah!"

But how do we do it? How do we even start such a daunting process? I fervently believe it starts with making one small moment in a rehearsal truly beautiful. One note, one measure, or one phrase. Once we get our students playing one tiny, lovely thing, we can then tell them how beautiful it was, and more importantly show them how emotionally touched we were. Words like: "Did you hear that? Play it again and *listen* to how beautiful it is. Just listen. That was gorgeous. It was simply breathtaking." That simple step is the start of teaching them it is okay to verbalize and physically show the extremes of human emotion. In that way our expression of those feelings can be true, not faked or staged, insincere or artificial. For undoubtedly, that would be worse than no emotion at all.

They must understand how powerful their music is. How music can give them the freedom to communicate their inner selves. It can be a way to share the thoughts and feelings of those they have never met and those they will never meet. It is emotion passed through time from generation to generation. We can look our students right in the eyes and ask them if they have ever met Johann Sebastian Bach. As one of his chorales sits on each of their music stands they will shake their heads with a confident no. To which we can reply, "Oh yes you have; you have his heart, mind, feelings, passions and thoughts on your music stands." We can ask them how that piece makes them feel. What they think a single note or phrase means. What words they would use to describe certain sounds. By truly performing that work they will come to know that as they hold that piece of music in their hands they are also holding the composer's soul.

There are those who will certainly disagree with this idea. It seems to me the trend over the past few years is for conductors to be more dispassionate. There are many who preach that emotion from the podium is to be avoided. In some circles the word emotion has become a four-letter word. Have we become so concerned about correctness as to be emotionally aloof? Though we are all entitled to our opinion, I have always lived by the words of Georg Wilhelm Friedrich Hegel who wrote, "We may affirm absolutely that nothing great in the world has been accomplished without passion."

Please know that in no way am I saying that we should be free to do anything we want. I am certainly not advocating overblown expressiveness or overbearing theatrics. If the portrayal of emotions gets in the way of a correct performance, all we have at the end of the day is nothing. If expressiveness is an excuse for incorrect playing the result can never be true emotions. The finest words I've ever read on this thought are those of renowned conductor George Szell. He succinctly stated, "The dualism of feeling and thinking must be resolved to a state of unity in which one thinks with the heart and feels with the brain." If we allow a technical passage to come only from the mind and be devoid of feelings from the heart it will be sterile and mechanical. If we allow expressive passages to come only from the heart without the restraint and taste held in our minds they will become so overly romantic as to be ridiculous. I liken this to fruit ripening on a tree. Eating an unripe apple is unsatisfying, but eating a piece of fruit, which has become so over-ripened with sweetness that it has turned rotten, is repulsive.

We can think of this like a dog on a leash. A short leash allows for a tense, harsh and militaristic walk. An overly long leash with far too much slack will give Fido the unbridled freedom to go wherever he wants, whether appropriate or not, allowing the owner absolutely no control. I believe the solution is to have a leash that is as long as possible, allowing for great expressive freedom; however, never so long as to foster a loss of control. A certain amount of freedom is necessary for self-expression and enjoyment.

The following quote, written by Bernard Shore describing the legendary conductor Sir Hamilton Hardy, goes a long way toward illustrating that of which we are capable: "In a wild passage his face becomes suffused with emotion, and without any great movement he obtains a terrific response from the players. He is fortunate in complete unselfconscious expression of his feelings. Nothing comes between him and the music he performs. Electricity he seems to be able to generate at will. One moment his sense of repose will fine everything down to the utmost tranquillity; then in a flash he can change the scene to one of wild orgy." Shore goes on to state that Harty's influence over a player gave "him a sense of artistry that he was not able or willing to put forth for any other conductor." Quite simply, we have to share with our students; we must lead them, with a score in one hand and a baton in the other. What *is* hiding in an empty box?

"Do or Do Not, There is No Try."

What a powerful phrase. Those words were spoken by that remarkable philosopher and teacher, Yoda, in the movie *Star Wars: The Empire Strikes Back,* during a scene at his home in the Dagoba System. Luke Skywalker was there to complete his training under Yoda's guidance. As the scene opens, Luke is doing a handstand. There standing on top of Luke's feet is Yoda. Luke is hard at work trying to make a large stone rise in the air, using only "the force." As Luke struggles, Yoda says to his young charge, "Use the force — yes. Now — the stone. Feel it." As Luke starts to lose control, and they begin to fall to the ground, Yoda exclaims, "Concentrate."

At that point, looking toward his X-Wing fighter stranded in the murky swamp near them, Luke sighs, "Oh no, we'll never get it out now." For in Luke's mind, the goal or only reason for doing that exercise was to right his ship. Calmly, Yoda says, "So certain are you. Always with you: it cannot be done. Do you nothing that I say?" More concerned with the goal than the ability, Luke replies, "Master, moving stones around is one thing. This is totally different." Growing more disappointed, Yoda states, "No, no different. Only different in your mind. You must unlearn what you have learned." Reluctantly and with a defeated sound in his voice, Luke replies, "Alright, I'll give it a try."

Now more frustrated and distressed, Yoda implores, "No, try not. Do, or do not — there is no try." Aiming his hand at the X-Wing buried in the swap, Luke intensely tries to make his craft rise in the air. Slowly, it starts to ascend a bit, but then falls back to the swamp. Both student and teacher sigh. Luke sits down near Yoda, and says, "I can't, it's too big." With growing impatience, Yoda replies, "Size matters not.

Look at me, judge me by my size do you, hmm? And where you should not, for my ally is the force. And a powerful ally it is. Life creates it, makes it grow. Its energy surrounds us, and binds us. Luminous beings are we, not this crude matter. You must feel the force around you. Here, between you — me — the tree, the rock, everywhere, yes even between land and the ship." Luke, now completely frustrated, responds by saying, "You want the impossible." With that said, Luke stands up and walks off a bit from his mentor.

As Luke sits back down, Yoda, with intense concentration, makes the ship rise in the air and places it gently on land. Luke watches in amazement. He walks over to the ship. He touches it. Then walking over to Yoda says, "I don't — I don't believe it." Without missing a beat, Yoda responds, "That is why you fail."

What an unlikely place to find wisdom. But wisdom nonetheless it is. Yoda knew. And from this parable we can learn so much. More certainly than meets the eye.

INFERENCE

In education, so much energy is spent on the concept of *trying*. The problem with our use of the word "trying" is we infer from it there can be two results, that of success or failure. In that way, if we do something, we either do it successfully and correctly, or we fail at doing it. The latter being thought of as a mistake. The opposite of doing is really *not doing* rather than failing. *Not doing* is simply the fact that we have not done something yet.

We project success or failure on our activities. Thus we are the author of our fulfillment. Robert Greene Ingersoll stated it so very clearly, "In nature, there are neither rewards nor punishments; there are consequences." Consequences are a result, a fact. Reward or punishment is all in our perception of what we have done. We cannot infer failure as a reaction to "do not." For if so, we imply that result is a mistake, something bad.

What then is a mistake? That word usually conjures up images of bad or incorrect. It is not. It is simply our perception of what we have done. If we, as Yoda put it "do" then we have done what we have sought to do. If we, again in his words "do not" we have not failed, we just haven't done it.

"Do or Do Not, There is no Try."

Do

Doing something is, in and of itself, succeeding. The final goal may not be reached. The result of our *doing* may not yet be what we want, but the act of doing is positive.

Frustration

With that way of thinking, our students should find much more patience with themselves. If we have students learning appropriate material in small enough steps, they can "do." Problems arise when we ask for what is not within the bounds of our students' readiness, do not systematically teach each step along the way, do not provide enough time for assimilating the skill, or work in such enormous steps as to make learning difficult.

Those issues create a sense of frustration for student and teacher. The goal is less often *too difficult* than it is *too big*, too far between steps rather than too many steps. Small steps allow students to regularly feel as though they can "do." If we make each small step along the path a goal able to be accomplished, we provide opportunities for feeling good, rather than creating frustration at how long it may take to get to the goal. Each stride in the process of *getting there* becomes *gotten there*. This goes a long way toward moving any wall of failure out of view, so it's less likely they will bang their heads on it. We decide what the "do" is to be.

Lots of small forward advances, able to be accomplished, create a sense of pride and fulfillment. Learning becomes far more positive and productive if attempts at "doing" something are considered: steps, practice, attempts at different approaches, the gaining of strength or the figuring out of a process. Frustration is often less about not seeing the goal, and more about not knowing the steps of how to get there.

We must let circumstances dictate our priorities, let priorities determine our actions, and not become overwhelmed by the task before us. We can't try to do *everything* all at once; we just have to do lots of little *somethings* headed toward it. As Oliver Wendell Holmes stated, "Where we stand is not so nearly as important as the direction we are moving."

Believe!

Poor Luke. Caught by his own words: "I don't believe it." Yoda's wisdom helped Luke to understand. Luke didn't believe in his own abilities *or* what was possible. Either can be destructive. To the former I say, if we believe, anything is possible. Or as Wayne Dyer once wrote, "You'll see it when you believe it." And to the latter, Cicero, the great philosopher held that one of *The Six Mistakes of Man* was "Insisting that a thing is impossible because we cannot accomplish it." When I think something not doable, I always remember the affirmation of Wernher von Braun, considered the father of the U. S. space program, "I have learned to use the word 'impossible' with the greatest caution."

UNLEARN

Yoda spoke of unlearning. It was not that the skill Luke had learned was wrong and needed to be unlearned, but that he had "learned" or convinced himself that either the task was impossible, or that he was incapable of doing it. It was his mindset that needed to be relearned! Yoda perceived it was Luke's attitude more than his ability that was standing in the way of his achievement. We have to convince our students of their capabilities, and that everything is possible. Difficulty is not impossibility.

UNIMAGINABLE

We must encourage our performers to realize they have no idea how far they can go. They can dream of the highest ambitions, strive for what is now incomprehensible. Granted, the higher the expectations the farther one can fall, but if each step is secure, anything is achievable. Will there be obstacles? Sure, but in the words of Frank A. Clark, "If you find a path with no obstacles, it probably doesn't lead anywhere." Anything is possible, obstacles and all. But as Yoda confirmed, we are often our own biggest obstacle. Our self-doubt can be staggering.

Though some doubt is part and parcel of being a musician, as described by Robert Hughes when he wrote, "The greater the artist, the greater the doubt; perfect confidence is granted to the less talented as a consolation prize." But to counter that I ask you to consider the words of the great Vincent van Gogh: "If you hear a voice within you say 'you cannot paint,' then by all means paint, and that voice will be silenced."

Paramount is getting our students to accept the inconceivable, expect the unimaginable, and achieve the impossible. Kevin McHale said it best, "It's not how good you are, it's how good you can become."

"...Find the Journey's End in Every Step..."

Those words of Ralph Waldo Emerson are as profound as any I know. We must enjoy each step of the journey as much as the destination. In the process of learning, each tiny stretch should be embraced and savored. Helping to develop an ensemble, teach a class or learn the clarinet is like turning a piece of wood on a lathe. If we jam the sculpting tool into the spinning wood in an effort to make fast progress, we will gouge the wood and probably ruin it. We patiently and methodically need to proceed in small increments.

But far more important is that we enjoy the process of teaching, and they of learning. Is our only satisfaction the finished product, or do we take pleasure in the unfolding of it? When eating a luscious steak dinner, is "getting it consumed" the object of our pleasure, or is enjoyment found in the savoring of every mouthful? Is emptying the bottle of a rare vintage wine where we find delight, or do we relish every sip? In that we really don't know how far our students can go, we must enjoy the path along the way, because we will never know when the *final* goal is at hand, or what it will be. In the words of a wonderful Indian proverb, "There is no one day where you can see a green apple turn into sweet fruit."

Turn Try Into Do, Doing, Done

Imagine sitting somewhere on the mainland shore looking out on the ocean. Just in sight is an island. That island of fulfillment is where we want our students to go. To the average person, there is no way to get there. No boat. Too far to swim. Impossible, they would think. That's because they are not teachers. We chase the dream of accomplishments, joy, realization and exhilaration for our students. We, as teachers, can see those "invisible" bridges leading to the island from any number of directions. But as with anything, those who can see, see. While those who cannot, say there is nothing to see, instead of taking the time to search for it. Using the wisdom of Yoda, what follows are a few of those bridges to help our students reach for and touch their goals.

POSSIBLE

We must believe that anything we know to be worthwhile and sound is possible. We need to make our students realize that with commitment, dedication and desire, the highest goals are within reach. As Helen Keller affirmed, "We can do anything we want to if we stick to it long enough." Our imagination is the only limit. William A. Ward once said, "If you can imagine it, you can achieve it. If you can dream it, you can become it." Underestimating is not realizing, as William Longgood wrote, that "Dreams and dedication are a powerful combination."

WE MUST INSPIRE

There is no doubt that knowledge is power. Equally true is that you can lead a horse to water, but not get him to drink. However, if you make that watering hole look like an oasis, he may be more inclined to take a sip! If we use the power of our personality to invigorate our students, they will be inspired to learn. Robert Frost wrote, "What is required is sight and insight — then you might add one more: excite." Seeing the music at hand is one thing. Knowing enough to offer insight into it is better. But being excited about it is the spark that will ignite the fire of our students' wanting to learn.

In *The Joy of Music*, the remarkable Leonard Bernstein wrote, "...the conductor must not only make his orchestra play; he must make them want to play. He must exalt them, lift them, start their adrenaline pouring...however he does it, he must make the orchestra love the music as he loves it. It is not so much imposing his will on them like a dictator; it is more like projecting his feelings around him so that they reach the last man in the second violin section."

When describing the characteristics of a conductor, Hector Berlioz stated, "It is essential that it should be felt that he feels, that he understands, that he is, as it were, 'possessed;' then his sentiment and his emotion communicate themselves to those whom he directs, the internal fire escapes him, his electricity electrifies them, the force of his impetus carries them away; he projects all around him the burning rays of the musical art."

David Ewen wrote that the conductor was "...the soul and life's breath of the orchestra, its dynamo of energy, its sensitized heart, its contemplative mind. He was now the medium between the music and the performers; and the music, as it coursed through his fingers, now began to acquire new depth, new shapes and new meanings." These descriptions can be us. We can inspire our students to do anything.

"DO OR DO NOT, THERE IS NO TRY."

DOING IS SUCCEEDING

Simply doing something toward the goal is an accomplishment. Not doing removes the fear of "failure" but it also eliminates any chance of moving forward. As John A. Shedd so masterfully stated, "A ship in harbor is safe — but that is not what ships are for." We have all heard that wonderful analogy to various sports: we miss *every* shot we don't take. When asked by students which of two paths they should follow, my usual answer is, "Yes." I don't know which will be best or more beneficial, but I do know that doing something is good. Inaction rarely leads to accomplishments.

THE MOTIVATION LOOP

Accomplishments, discipline and motivation work to create a wonderfully complimentary cycle. That *Motivation Loop* consists of four parts. First, if our rehearsals are disciplined, focused, rigorous and controlled they will be productive and positive. Second, if that is the case, it will allow for a clear, unified expression by the ensemble and a canvas for their personal expression. Third, if that is true, it creates excitement, thrills, chills, tingles-up-the-spine, tears and emotions. Fourth, that makes our students want to do more, get better, achieve even higher heights and jump hurdles they can't yet even see. With each pass of this loop we reinforce positive growth and our faith in their abilities, as well as confirm the joys of hard work and effort.

WE ARE AS WE ARE THOUGHT TO BE

Those words may seem like I'm saying we should walk off the mainland toward that island armed with only the *hope* that our *belief* in a bridge will produce one. I'm not, well, not completely. As much as that would be crazy, I do believe that *how we act* is often as important as what we do. As Goethe asserted, "If you treat an individual as he is, he will stay as he is. But if you treat an individual the way he ought to be, he will become what he ought to be and could be." In the words of Mahatma Gandhi, "You must be the change you wish to see in the world." So, as the old saying prescribes, "Act as if the quality you seek is already within you and it will be." If we act the way we want to act, we *will* be acting the way we want to be acting. If we treat students as if they are acting the way we wish them to, often they will.

No Obstacle Is Too Great

An obstacle is an obstacle. However, it is how it is viewed that makes the difference. It can be thought to stop us, thus preventing our ability to move forward in any way. It can be seen as weighing us down or slowing, rather than halting, our progress toward the goal. But, it can also be interpreted as an opportunity to use creativity and imagination. I know that sounds like optimism gone amuck, but we all know it's true! The story I always tell when I think an ensemble believes more in an obstacle's ability to stop them than their ability to overcome it, is about the legendary Itzhak Perlman.

Jack Reimer, as written in the *Houston Chronicle*, reported about a concert the renowned violinist gave at Lincoln Center in New York City. Reimer poignantly tells of Perlman coming on stage, readying himself, motioning to the conductor to begin, and starting the performance. Within seconds, like "gunfire," all could hear one of Perlman's strings break. As the performance stopped, everyone in attendance wondered what would happen next.

Reimer writes, "...he waited a moment, closed his eyes and then signaled the conductor to begin again. The orchestra began, and he played from where he had left off. And he played with such passion and such power and such purity as they had never heard before. Of course, anyone knows that it is impossible to play a symphonic work with just three strings. I know that, and you know that, but that night Itzhak Perlman refused to know that."

Reimer describes overwhelming applause for the soloist after the work ended. He then goes on to state that Perlman "...smiled, wiped the sweat from his brow, raised his bow to quiet us, and then he said, not boastfully, but in a quiet, pensive, reverent tone, 'You know, sometimes it is the artist's task to find out how much music you can still make with what you have left.'"

When I think of that story, obstacles seem to gain perspective, and the ability for human beings to overcome obstacles grows immensely. We just have to convince ourselves and our students of that *fact*. As Ernest Hemingway wrote, "Think what you can do with what there is."

There Is No Time Like Now

A fantastic African proverb reminds us that "The best time to plant a tree is twenty years ago, the next best time is today." We are dealt a hand of cards, we may wish that it contains four aces, but if it doesn't we need to work with what we are given toward that end. Today is the foundation of the future. "If we don't change the direction we are going," a Chinese proverb suggests, "we are likely to end up where we are heading."

BACKWARDS COMPLETION PRINCIPLE

This simple theory proposes that one way to figure out the steps to a goal is to envision the moment of its completion, and then work backwards to see how you got there. Sometimes thinking this way offers insights for getting to the goal you would not have imagined otherwise. Using your imagination to think through the progression from the goal back to the starting place also offers an opportunity to think about what you could do differently, what should be changed, or what could be made better or easier along that path. Sometimes viewing our situation from another angle, in this case backwards, allows for clearer vision.

TEACH CURIOSITY

Though we have all heard the following quote, it helps us never to lose sight of the mark. "You can teach a lesson for a day, but if you teach curiosity, you teach for a lifetime." Getting our students to wonder, ponder and debate is wonderful. Getting them to want to search for knowledge is even better. Inspiring them to question any thought that they have reached a plateau of learning is even better still.

NEVER UNDERESTIMATE

Some time ago, I was working with an ensemble on a piece that allowed for a great deal of rubato. I asked the ensemble to work to create a very expressive portrayal. Just before the concert, their director came up to me and said, "You really like to gamble, don't you." We both agreed that playing that piece without rubato would have been the sanest way to go. I didn't. If I hadn't had them "reach for the brass ring" they would have missed the chance to experience the expression of those emotions. Even more importantly, I did not want them to think for a minute I had any doubt about their ability. We need to help young people anticipate greatness, envision wonder, and foresee better than we can imagine. Never underestimate the power of music or our students. Sometimes taking a chance isn't really taking a chance at all.

LET GO OF BAGGAGE

Often it is the weight of *believing* we can't do something that must be "unlearned." That baggage we take with us along the path toward our goal is sometimes the most important thing to be changed. If we teach ourselves something is impossible, and continue to reinforce it, it will be. We must learn to ignore that encumbrance, for it can be of no help to anyone. Henry Ford may have said it best when he remarked, "Whether you think you can or think you can't — you are right."

NONCHALANCE

Sometimes "trying too hard" can be our undoing. If we work toward ability and understanding that is unfettered by worry, concern and angst, we often will be at our best. As Eugen Herrigel stated in *Zen in the Art of Archery,* "The swordmaster is as unself-conscious as the beginner. The nonchalance which he forfeited at the beginning of his instruction he wins back again at the end as an indestructible characteristic." Remember the reckless abandon with which you played your trumpet when you were a beginner? Do you still play with that freedom?

As you watch great artists in performance, are you struck by how easy they make it look? It seems as effortless as breathing. To them it is. They have come full circle. As a beginner they undoubtedly played with not a care in the world. As they began to study, more than likely they added worry and concern to their approach. "Trying" does that. It is only when skill allows for confidence that we can return to those carefree ways, now armed with and fueled by true mastery.

Often as we "learn" we become thwarted by worry of correctness and technique. Once we feel we truly know something, we are freed to allow ourselves to use it with ease. We then are no longer bogged down by the shackles of effort but are free to allow the application of the skill to be nonchalant.

TEACH ASPIRATION

At a band festival rehearsal I was conducting some time ago, the ensemble was working on a composition that had the French horns, in unison, playing a slow, soft, elegant melody that leaped to the stratosphere several times. After the first playing, I said, "Please French horns, that beautiful melody can have no cracks, must be pianissimo, smooth, effortless sounding, in tune and be molto legato." To which one of the horn players questioned, "That's all, you don't want world

"DO OR DO NOT, THERE IS NO TRY."

peace too?" Of course I responded with the only retort possible: "Okay, throw in an order of world peace." Not to be outdone by his conductor, the horn player's response was, "Will you settle for an end to global warming?" After wiping the tears of laughter from my eyes, we went to work. That melody wasn't always great, but we worked to get as close to the goal as possible, never settling to work toward less.

The following poem always reminds me of our task. I have always known it to be anonymous. I wish I knew who wrote it, so I could tell that person how much it means to me.

> The teacher said to the students,
> "Come to the edge."
> They replied,
> "We may fall."

> The teacher again said,
> "Come to the edge,"
> and they responded,
> "It's too high."

> "Come to the edge"
> the teacher demanded
> and they came
> and the teacher pushed them
> and they flew.

THOSE WHO *CAN* — TEACH

It was near the end of my first semester of college. I had just completed a seminar for all freshmen music education majors. Every Friday afternoon we gathered to talk about the prospect of teaching music. We would share stories, ask questions, and try to figure out what we would need to know by the time we graduated. With every story and comment my fear and trepidation grew. Would I ever be capable of knowing enough to teach music? Just before final exams I made an appointment to see my advisor, who happened to be the chair of the music education department and the teacher of that seminar. As I sat in his office he calmly asked what I was there to discuss. That wonderful, kind and remarkable gentleman sat and listened as I said, "I don't think I can do it." "Do what?" he asked. "Be a music teacher," I replied.

He then took a deep breath, crossed his arms, sat back in his chair and asked with a knowing and fatherly expression on his face, "Tell me why you think that." I went on to say, "I'll never know enough to do it. With so many people who want to teach music, how will I ever get a job?" My advisor thought for a moment and with a reassuring smile said, "There's always room at the top." He went on to say that the best in any profession would be sought out. Hard work, passion and dedication would provide what is needed to be good enough to be *allowed* to teach young people music. He never promised me a job. Never told me I would be good enough. Gave me no shallow motivational pep talk. He simply made it clear how important music teaching was and how good you had to be to *deserve* that title. He gave me a lot to think about. And though I continued to question my abilities, I never questioned my desire. His statement was so powerful.

Some years later at a conference, I found myself in a conversation with several professors of music. Over lunch, in a heated discussion about the worth of music education as an academic discipline, one of them said, "Let us never lose sight of the fact that those who can *do*, and those who can't *teach*!" I sat speechless. I couldn't even defend my discipline. I could hardly move. It was like someone had punched me. But it wasn't that I was offended by what he said. I was shaken by what he said. He made me more uncomfortable than angry. More bewildered than belligerent. At that moment, I sat back as thoughts flooded my head. It was the oddest experience. As I sat listening to those gentlemen almost yelling at each other, quiet thoughts started roaming around in my mind. It was like a scene from a bad television sitcom.

Throughout my life I had heard that awful sentiment about teaching. I had always just ignored it. I simply used the "sticks and stones" rationalization. But on that occasion, my advisor's statement and that professor's comment waged all-out war in my mind. My beliefs were shaken to their very foundation. I could go on for pages and not truly describe to you how baffled I was. For the first time in my life I actually *thought* about that horrid expression. Was it simply that I wasn't good enough to make a living as a performing musician, so teaching was the next best thing? Was what I did in some unspoken way simply a fallback to the next closest occupation?

As the weeks passed, I found myself watching my colleagues and myself with great scrutiny. I thought about what we did, and why we did it. I knew how absurd that sentiment was, but for the first time, I simply could not let go of it by ignoring it. I had to come to terms with *why* it was ridiculous. It drove me crazy. I couldn't shake it. Then it came to me. Inherent in that sentiment is that the goal of music education must be to *produce* professional performers. That is, for those who share that professor's opinion, *those who can*. The shortsightedness of that thought is it presumes all we teach is how to perform music. It ignores the fact that what we really teach is living, emoting, coping, striving, cooperating and imagining. The essence of the clash between that professor's comment and my advisor's statement was that the professor's comment assumed that the goal was a *product*: the professional performer. Whereas my advisor's words came from the knowledge of what all teachers know: the goal is the *process*, the journey along the way, not where we land. That was the crux of the gap between those two notions. I finally understood.

I was so happy I was able to come to terms with that terrible adage. I now realized *how*, but more importantly *why* it was so absurd. I wanted to start a national ad campaign to dispute it. I'm not sure which aspect of that old saw bothered me more, the ridiculous notion that performing music at a professional level and teaching music are mutually exclusive, or that our collective purpose is simply to produce professional performers. We all know why we teach music. We teach because we love sharing our art with young people and helping them develop in as many different ways as there are colors in the rainbow.

That wrestling match in my mind made my resolve for what we do even stronger. But it also made me step back and think about my chosen profession, and the temperament needed for those who choose to rise to its challenges. I started to think of various occupations and how the philosophies and dispositions needed for other careers would work if they were applied to music teaching. More importantly, it made me think of how "process versus product" affects different occupations. How would professionals in other fields teach music if bound by that professor's single goal of developing professional performers? Thus began my stream of consciousness, a flight of fancy, a parody about imagined stereotypes!

The first job I thought about was that of a corporate CEO. My observation of that career path has a person stepping into that position in a large, well-developed and ongoing company. She is charged with either making it profitable or seeing that it remains profitable. So often it seems she stays for a short while and then moves on to another ongoing major corporation. Her success or failure is judged on the profitability of her corporation. It is all about product. If we were to use that model for music teaching, it would be like deciding we would only coach current members of the New York Philharmonic. Though they may be playing the best they ever had, or be in a bit of a slump, nonetheless they are already hugely successful and able. I can just hear a CEO as a music teacher addressing a fourth-grade beginner orchestra: "Today we will start working on Beethoven's Fifth Symphony. By the deadline for the fourth quarterly report we must have it to a professional performance level or I will have to leave and teach another orchestra."

The second career I looked at was that of an investment banker. It seemed to me that he would decide to invest in a startup company only after it showed evidence of viability and future profitability. He has little interest in any company that does not seem destined for huge monetary gains. If we were to use that as a corollary for music teaching, we would need to walk into our class of beginning fourth-grade flute players and assess their aptitude. Then we would only teach those who could prove to us beyond a shadow of a doubt that their future would have them sit in the Chicago Symphony flute section. They would somehow have to prove that now. Without that proof, we would not provide them instruction. Can't you just hear the investment banker music teacher saying to a group of fourth-graders, "Now who can provide documentation that you will eventually sit in the Chicago Symphony? If any of you can, then I will be glad to start you on flute lessons."

I then thought about the career of a surgeon. She receives a problem and acts upon it. Almost immediately, she will know whether the operation was a success or a failure. What is done in the operating room either worked or didn't. For the music teacher, this would be like having one and only one lesson with a beginner. By the end of that lesson they would either know enough to land a job playing professionally, or not. In the course of that one very finite period of time we would succeed or fail. From the surgeon music teacher we might hear: "My diagnosis is that none of you fourth-graders, having never held a clarinet before, currently knows how to play the clarinet. You need to assemble the instrument and mouthpiece like this, then produce a sound as follows. Come back and see me in six weeks and we can see if you are playing well enough to perform with the New York Philharmonic. If not, you and your family have my deepest sympathy."

I then moved on to think about farmers. They plant seeds, tend to the land and nurture their crop from beginning to end. The beauty of what they do is that in a very short period of time they see their harvest, the efforts of their labor in its totality. If they plant tomatoes, in a precious few weeks they end up eating beautiful ripe tomatoes in their completely grown state. If we were to liken this to teaching music, we would have to start beginners on an instrument knowing we would need them ready for the Boston Symphony in three months. The farmer music teacher would have the following discussion with his fourth-grade band: "Today I'm going to teach you how to play the trombone. I'm going to help you with every aspect of your growth. But in three months, with good weather, I'll be sending you off to the Boston Symphony, so you better be completely, fully developed and ready to perform at a professional level by that harvest date."

Next, I thought of the job of marine biologists at a shelter for injured sea animals. (How's that for a stream of consciousness!) They receive an animal, take as long as is necessary to nurture it back to health, and then release it back into the wild with hopes of health and well-being. Though they never really know the final outcome of their labors, they know the animal is well and healthy *before* sending it off into the world. If we were to use that as a model for teaching music, we would start young people in elementary school and not let them leave school until they were ready for the Cleveland Orchestra. For the marine biologist music teacher it would go something like this: "Jimmy, I am going to keep teaching you until you can play at a professional level. I don't care how long it takes, I'll be keeping you here in fifth grade until you are ready for the Cleveland Orchestra, then hopefully by the time you're twenty, off you go to sixth grade."

Next, I thought about architects. They dream of an idea, figure out how to make it possible, then in its totality pass it on to others to make it into reality. Certainly the beauty of this occupation is that they eventually get to see their finished product. For a music teacher, that would be like deciding how you envision a professional ensemble's performance of a certain work. You design a performance that will thrill thousands, but ask others to teach the students, and get them to that professional performance level. The architect music teacher would say, "Welcome, everyone, to the first rehearsal of the middle school band. I have envisioned and dreamt of how you should perform *The Stars and Stripes Forever*. Mr. Smith, your science teacher, will be teaching you how to perform the work to my expectations. I'll be looking forward to hearing your performance to see how it turns out."

Please don't get me wrong, I'm not saying that one profession should be thought of as better than another. Heaven knows I'm glad we have dedicated professionals in all of the above-mentioned career paths. I am simply taking note of different tendencies, expectations, and traits that might go along with different professions, and applying that professor's ludicrous goal to each of them. As silly as they are, those thoughts do point out how different occupations could deal with the idea of process versus product, and making the latter the goal.

So how do we describe our profession? What is our product? We don't move a company to profitability, remove a diseased organ from a person, nurse an injured whale back to health, grow crops to feed a community, design a bridge to be built, or find venture capital for a fledgling company. We might not cure a person from sickness, feed a hungry village, save a company from failure, plant a forest, create jobs for the downtrodden, invent a vaccine, defend the innocent, govern a people, command an army, rescue a crew, or build a building. No, we probably won't. But in how we affect the hearts and minds of our students, from the lives we touch and the lives they will touch, a teacher lives for eternity and does all manner of great things. We are all about the process, not the final product! A chef cooks for a meal, an olympian wins for an instant, an engineer builds for a project, a sailor sails for a voyage, a pilot flies for a flight, a surgeon cures for a lifetime, but we as teachers are *forever.*

We are teachers — we invest our time, energy, talents, encouragement, dedication, patience, passion and commitment. Why? To train people to have music in their lives. Not necessarily as a career, but to sit on school boards and support music education. To be a member of a community and vote their support of music education. To sing in a community chorus. To buy tickets to hear a professional orchestra. To encourage their children on the day they come home from fourth grade and say, "Mom, I want to play the trumpet!" We don't teach for ourselves — but as a gift to our students, a gift to our art, and a gift to future generations that we'll never know. As Neil Postman wrote, "Children are the living messages we send to a time we will not see."

We don't just teach the art and science of music with its enormous crossover to other subjects, and the concomitant benefits to student achievement. We enrich the spirit, develop the mind, feed the heart, soothe the soul, nurture the character, unleash the emotions, and instill pride in young people. If, as Erich Fromm said, "Man's main task in life is to give birth to himself," then in my opinion, his second task must be to help others give birth to themselves. A teacher knows his or her students as they were, sees them as they are, and envisions them as they will become. Regular people see students as they *are* at this moment, but teachers see them as they *can be* in the future. We change lives for the better. As Rodger Austin wrote, "Sometimes people, who come into your life, make changes in you. Because you always take a little part of them with you into the future. We are all made up of little bits and pieces of those whose lives touch ours." We as teachers touch the lives of all those we guide. In that way, we truly live for eternity.

Do we matter? Do we really matter? Zoltán Kodály wrote, "Real art is one of the most powerful forces in the rise of mankind and he who renders it accessible to as many people as possible is a benefactor of humanity." If you can teach young people to sing what you will never sing, hear what you will never hear, appreciate what you will never know, play what you will never play, and dream what you will never dream, then you will have made a difference. You will have been that benefactor of humanity. Yes, it can be frustrating and tiring, and sometimes it does feel like our occupation, using the words of Ernest Newman, is "...a combination of the hypnotist and the lion-tamer." But we know how important, how truly important, teaching music is.

We give students wings and help them to fly. Can't you just close your eyes and see the faces of all of those students from years past taking flight? Do you know why there is "always room at the top" for music teachers? Because that's the best place from which to sit quietly, look to the skies, smile knowingly, and watch them *soar*. It seems so clear to me now. That old saw was close. It has simply been passed down a bit incorrectly. How should it read? Those who *can't* — don't. Those who *can* — teach!

"If You Don't Know, I Can't Tell You!"

That's not a very reassuring title for the person about to embark on reading this chapter. You're probably wondering why there are any words on this page at all. It makes me think of one of those speeches given at a banquet. You know, where after eating dinner, the guest speaker is brought to the dais and asked to share everything he knows with all who are gathered. Now picture if on that banquet program you were to see the words used for this chapter title. You would probably expect the speaker to stand at the lectern, graciously receive the applause, and then begin his speech by firmly saying, "Thank you very much. I can't tell you anything, so I'm going to sit down now," as he went back to his place at the head table. If you've been to as many banquets as I have, you would undoubtedly agree that would be followed by raucous applause as all in attendance looked around in shock saying, "Now that is how all banquet speeches should be." My experience with dinner speeches all too often has the speaker rant on for thirty minutes or so. Then, as he comes up for air, he utters those words that can make a grown man or woman cry: "Now for the *second* half of my speech...." Those scenes aside, it does seem a bit odd that a chapter with the above title would be longer than one sentence. I can imagine you're thinking: "If he can't tell me something, why is he going on for pages?" Let me try to explain.

The past few years have brought a flurry of interest in and discussion about learning standards, advocacy and justifying the place of music in modern education. Those topics are indeed pressing and of great significance. Though they have always been of concern, they seem to have risen to new heights of timeliness and importance. Just like most music teachers, I have spent the better part of my career defending music as an integral part of a person's education. Over the years of preaching that, we have all gathered vast bits of ammunition about why music should hold its rightful place in the curriculum. Though some may be truer than others, we have all heard those snippets of information about how music helps an individual. Statements like music helps to raise math, foreign language, reading and SAT scores. It helps a person develop eye-hand coordination, self-esteem, self-expression, voice inflection, creativity, imagination and self-discipline. Music helps students learn fractions, problem solving, acoustics as well as about events and cultures throughout history. In addition, we help students learn to deal with their emotions, and experience that almost unexplainable feeling of esprit de corps. The list goes on and on. And the truth be known, every time I hear one of those thoughts disputed, even if supported by statistics, I can't help but believe all of them are still true. With all we know music *does* do, all the testaments from people about how important music has been in their lives, and with all the joy music has brought the world, our defense of music should be so unnecessary. Why do we have to justify what we do? It seems so obvious to *me*. It seems so simple. I then remembered the words of H. L. Mencken when he stated, "For every complex problem, there is a solution that is simple, neat, and wrong."

So why do we have to defend music education? Do English teachers have to defend their place in the curriculum? Do math teachers always feel their subject is at risk for cuts in staffing, scheduling or budget? Do science teachers spend time worrying about keeping their subject as part of the core of what is taught to young people? Like you, music has always been the most important part of my educational life. *We* could not imagine *our* world without music. So I wanted to know why. Why do we have to defend our subject?

I decided I would listen to the arguments against us. I started with that question we have all heard about vocation versus avocation, those pearls of wisdom about how few of our students will become full-time professional musicians, thus making a vocation of their study. Without question that is true. But how many of our physical education students will become professional quarterbacks or pitchers? How many of us have ever used a microscope at our job? Obviously that argument is ridiculous. We agree that all of what a young person learns goes to making him or her well rounded, learned and experienced. As James Truslow Adams stated, "There are obviously two educations. One should teach us how to make a living and the other how to live."

All too often the second argument we hear is how expensive music is to teach. That is true. When you look at the cost of buying music stands, instruments, performance music and the like, we are expensive. But when we compare what is spent on music to that which is spent on athletic teams and science labs, music is a bargain. Please don't get me wrong, I am not in any way trying to attack other subjects whose place is more secure in our current educational value system. I simply am trying to make the point that any argument used against music can be used against many other subjects that seemingly are valued more by many.

After thinking about those arguments, I still had no more of an answer than when I started. So I decided I would study great thinkers. They would undoubtedly have the answers I sought. I reread the works of Socrates and Aristotle. I went back and studied the quadrivium and trivium. Those tenets, still remarkable today, firmly stated that music was essential in a person's education. I studied the works of Plato and his strong thoughts about music education. Plato — one of the great thinkers of all time stated, "Music is a moral law. It gives a soul to the universe, wings to the mind, flight to the imagination, a charm to sadness, gaiety and life to everything. It is the essence of order, and leads to all that is good, just and beautiful, of which it is invisible, but nevertheless dazzling, passionate and eternal form." I don't know which is more amazing to me: that that remarkable human being could have expressed it so well, or that other human beings could be so oblivious to its truth. For those who still don't believe how important Plato thought music to be, he stated it even more clearly and succinctly when he said, "Music is to the mind as air is to the body." After reading what those brilliant individuals thought, I was more puzzled than ever as to how any one could still question our art. The answer seemed even more elusive.

I decided my next step should be to study great educators. I read the thoughts of John Amos Comenius, the father of modern education and his work represented in *The Great Didactic*. That extraordinary gentleman gave us so much in the way of teaching techniques and principles of education. I went back and studied the work of Lowell Mason, who many feel was the father of modern music education. After studying countless numbers of his books in the collection of the Boston Public Library, I was reminded of the impact he had on music, but more importantly the impact music, he felt, had on him and his students. It was so clear to me. Why wasn't it that clear to everyone who questioned music's place in education? How could we defend music in a way all would understand?

I continued my quest by studying the writings of great musician-educators such as Paul Hindemith, Carl Orff and Zoltán Kodály. I read each of their thoughts on how important music and music education was for every person. Whether it was Hindemith's advocacy of Gebrauchsmusik, Orff's *Schulwerk* or Kodály's teachings, they all were interested in music for life. They weren't concerned about grooming the next concertmistress of the Boston Symphony or the next lead trumpet player for a Broadway musical. Though each of them had risen to the level of great success in their own professional musical careers, they were concerned about the common person. They felt music had to have a place in everyone's life. To them music as an avocation was even more important than music as a vocation. They truly thought that the joy brought by music to one's life in all manner of ways unexplainable was certainly something every person was owed by his or her guardians. When viewed with the power it can have in people's lives, the impact music teachers have is somewhat frightening.

We as music teachers have an obligation to civilization and to its people. As Kodály wrote, the administrator of an opera house is far less important than the music teacher in a school. The administrator's failure does have impact. But, in his words, "...a bad teacher may kill off the love of music for thirty years from thirty classes of pupils." If we extrapolate from that sentiment, the damage is even more far reaching. The student of that bad teacher, having had poor training and thus an inferior experience in music, will more than likely bring that disposition to his or her children, and they to theirs, and they to theirs. In that way, generations of children to come will lose that incredibly important facet of their growth and education as human beings.

Now with an even greater sense of debilitating frustration, I realized I still had no answer as to why it was so clear to me and seemingly so unclear to many who questioned the importance of music in education. We obviously must not be explaining it very well. I needed someone wiser than Socrates and Aristotle. Someone more enlightened than Plato and Comenius. Someone more insightful than Mason and Hindemith. Someone more learned than Orff and Kodály. Then it hit me: I remembered back to my first teaching experience. Working with an extremely experienced and wonderful gentleman, I was teaching seventh-grade instrumental music. Before the bell rang on my first day, we sat in the music office drinking coffee. I was so excited. Do you remember how excited you were on that first day? I was almost trembling in anticipation. I was about to work with young people. My dream of sharing my love of music with children was about to be realized. I could hardly contain myself. As we sat there chatting, I heard the sound of a trumpet coming from the band room. Like a Pavlovian dog hearing a bell ring, my adrenaline started to flow! It was clear to me that this young person had come in before school started in order to practice. Immediately, I asked if I should go in and work with him. I was told very calmly that it probably wasn't a good idea. Truly puzzled, but not wanting to rock the boat on my first morning, I sat and drank my coffee while that experienced teacher worked with the student.

The next morning, the scene was replayed. Again, I was told it probably wasn't a good idea for me to go into the band room and work with that young person. By the third morning, I couldn't stand it anymore. I wandered into the band room. There I met a seventh-grade boy by the name of Billy. I asked Billy if he wanted a lesson. He and I spent about twenty minutes that morning working on his trumpet playing. He was a delightful young man. He was very attentive and seemed mature beyond his years. After a few minutes of working with Billy I noticed that the way in which he lifted the trumpet up before he played appeared to be awkward. It seemed to be with more effort than it should have been. Just before the first bell rang we ended our session and I sent him on his way.

A few days later, as I sat drinking my coffee before school, I again heard the sound of a trumpet. I walked into the band room, and there was Billy. From then on, we worked together most every morning. Over time I realized his odd manner of lifting the trumpet was becoming more labored. With each passing day the movement seemed more filled with effort and discomfort. Eventually it became clear to me that Billy was starting to feel pain each time he lifted his horn. Speaking with other teachers, I was told what I was seeing was a manifestation of the fact that Billy had muscular dystrophy. It seemed his muscles grew tired each time he brought the instrument to his lips. I also came to find out that was why I was advised against working so closely with Billy. No one knew how long he would be with us. As the weeks passed, the energy expended by Billy to play the trumpet was exhausting. It had far less to do with producing a sound than it did with simply hold-ing the instrument up.

My feelings of helplessness grew with Billy's feelings of frustration and fatigue. But he never gave up. He never stopped loving his mu-sic. It seemed that no frustration would stop him. As months passed it got to the point where Billy would start with the trumpet on his lap, clutching it with both hands. He would then gather up all the power and strength he possessed, and with one burst he would thrust the trumpet up so that the bell was pointing straight into the air. Then as if cushioned with an open parachute, the trumpet started to come down to its normal placement in a slow descent while at the same time Billy set his lips upon the mouthpiece. He would then have a window of op-portunity during which he could play his trumpet: from where the bell was just above the horizon until it fell to his lap. The frustration grew to be palpable. I didn't know how to help him.

The first morning of school after the December vacation, I again heard Billy playing his trumpet in the band room. I walked into the room and there he was seated behind some contraption. Watching Billy play over the vacation, his grandfather realized he knew how to help. He took a Christmas tree stand; you know that metal bowl with feet and screws to hold an evergreen in place. He then bent a coat hanger and fashioned a large "V" to act as a holster for the bell of the trumpet. That was attached to the top of a length of two-by-four lumber. The wood was inserted into the stand like the base of a tree. With a few adjustments for height, Billy was ready to go. He would sit behind that gizmo, gather his strength for one good burst of energy, lift the bell in the air, and have it land in the coat-hanger holster. It was brilliant. His grandfather saw a problem and found the solution. Now the bottom of that bell did get a bit banged up, but Billy was playing his trumpet with renewed zeal!

It worked so well. But even that couldn't stop the muscles from growing weaker. As time passed, it grew harder and harder for Billy to play his trumpet. It seemed so painful. During one such time in a lesson I asked Billy if he wanted to keep going. He nodded yes. At that mo-ment, I finally gathered the courage to ask him the question that had been on my mind for months. I looked him in the eye and said, "Billy, I have to ask you a question." He said, "What?" I replied, "Why do you do it?" Quite puzzled he said, "Do what?" Gathering my composure I asked, "Why do you still want to play the trumpet so much even though it's causing you such pain?" He turned his head toward me, looked up at me, stared me right in the eyes and said, "Mr. Boonshaft, if you don't know, I can't tell you!" I stood there dumbfounded. I kept replaying those words over in my head. It was utterly amazing. The power of that simple statement has never left my mind or my heart. He knew. I realized then what that little seventh-grader knew all along. He knew words were useless. He was as wise as he was courageous and sincere. Billy expressed in words the inexpressible. He saw the invisible. He heard the inaudible. He knew what words could not express. That little twelve-year-old boy understood.

Remembering what Billy had taught me, I realized that the real reason I couldn't answer my *original* question was that I couldn't put the answer into words that everyone could understand. The problem to me was like trying to describe the *Mona Lisa* in five easy words or less. It was like trying to describe the taste of a wonderful vintage port, the impact of a sunset, or the birth of a child. No wonder those great people in history could never really describe why music was so important. They could only describe the impact it had on them and others. We are trying to use words to describe the indescribable.

I saw a commercial on television once. It was aired only months after the devastating attacks of 11 September 2001 on the United States of America. The commercial showed a team of those magnificent Clydesdale horses walking toward the City of New York from a great distance across a snow-covered field. As the Statue of Liberty and New York City skyline came into sight, the horses stopped, looked at what was before them, and were seen to bow. No words were spoken; no text was written. Only a group of horses bowing in reverence. I sat watching with tears in my eyes. But as powerful as that sight was, what gave it true expression, what took it to the core of every person who watched, was the impassioned and intense music with which it was accompanied. It would have been a beautiful sight in silence. With music, however, it was magnificent and awe-inspiring. The problem we have is that we can talk about the power of music until we are blue in the face. We can discuss and preach. But I think we can all agree that the only way people will truly understand *why*, is to experience it and be touched by it.

But what is the "it?" That was now the question I had. Is it simply to hear music or perform music? Of course not. The former happens to everyone in any elevator. The latter happens to so many. Sadly though, for a great number of people it is for such a short amount of time as to have little impact. In the preceding ways, virtually every person alive has come in contact with music. So why wouldn't all agree with its importance in education? If all we had to do to get people to come to know the virtues of music was to expose them to it, we should be "preaching to the choir" when we defend our art. So where are things breaking down?

I believe the problem is that to get to our goal as advocates, many of us are too worried about quantity. We want every one to experience and appreciate what we love. We believe the more people we can impact the better. To some extent that may help, but I believe if we are to truly convince the masses we must be far more concerned with quality. The impact we desire can only be true and long-lasting if it is through excellence. Experiencing music that is poorly performed can't bring performer or listener to come to know the greatness of our art. Don't get me wrong, advocacy is important. It's just that I believe so many advocacy efforts fail because their focus is on getting a lot of people to experience music rather than experience excellence in music. Mediocrity won't work; only excellence does. So much attention is paid to the numbers game. I'm as guilty as anyone is, but we have to know in our hearts that *big* is not necessarily good; big is big, good is good. The path to appreciating and valuing music is through coming to know its power: the power of music played so well as to evoke emotions from listener and performer alike. Through excellence in the performance of music, students will be allowed to experience the indescribable: the emotion, passion, power, beauty and expression of music. It is that quality that brings a listener and performer to experience tears of joy.

But as Plato knew, what music offers is so very much more. We don't just teach music, we teach excellence in everything through music. Our purpose is to help young people find happiness in their lives. To experience heights of emotion and thrills of success. To understand that through excellence in doing anything comes the reward of its virtues. To that end, we need to continue to teach, and expose our students to, musical excellence. We must strive for ever greater heights for our students and for ourselves. In that way we will grow, and our students will grow. We must be our students' guide, the pacesetter, the standard bearer for excellence. Not just for their *music education*, but for their *education in living*.

When thinking of that aspiration, I often remember a quote that was handed to me on a piece of paper at the end of a session I gave years ago: "Excellence is the result of caring more than others think is wise; risking more than others think is safe. Dreaming more than others think is practical, and expecting more than others think is possible." We touch our students deeply. We touch them profoundly. We help them enjoy living, not just existing. We help them to appreciate the beautiful in art, drama, dance, architecture, music, poetry, and all other manner of life. Every music teacher is like a lighthouse. We don't just offer a light for some to see by, but a torch, a magnificent torch. It may be invisible to some, but it is a beacon for all to follow. We must simply help everyone follow that light.

Why can't we put it into words? Why can't we describe the capacity of musical excellence? Why can't we really explain to everyone why music is so important to life? I think Carlyle said it best when he wrote, "Who is there that in logical words can express the effect music has on us? A kind of inarticulate, unfathomable speech, which leads us to the edge of the infinite, and lets us for moments gaze into that!"

Billy knew. All these years later, he is often on my mind, always in my heart and forever in my soul. See — I couldn't tell you.

POSTLUDE:
A LIE, THE FUTURE
AND A PUPPETEER

An unlikely trio of words. Do you know what *they* have in common? They each represent a quote that guides me everyday as a teacher. Three simple phrases, each of which is capable of making me tremble at the awesome responsibility we have, marvel at the wonder that is our art, and cry with elation at the utter joy we help share. They remind me of how proud we can be of what we do. We teach music. Or do we?

What we really teach is an illusion. It is as fake as can be. For you see, what we actually teach is a lie. As Picasso said, "Art is a lie that makes us realize the truth." Music is just that. It is a mirage. We teach that illusion to help students rise to heights of expression and emotion that allow them to know the truth: the beauty and wonder that is them and their world. *That* is the truth. Music is just a lie that facilitates that knowledge.

We as teachers are inextricably linked to our music, our students, our world and humanity. We collectively hold the future of our young people, thus our art and world, in our hands. Our students' happiness, understanding, passions, and experiences are our responsibility. The future truly is ours. We can shape the reality to come. Let us never forget the words of Peter F. Drucker: "The best way to predict the future is to create it."

In an earlier chapter, I talked about listening to a speech by the remarkable educator and entertainer Shari Lewis. As I listened to each passing word, I became ever more electrified by her thoughts. I can think of no better way to close this book than to share the simple power of a phrase she spoke that day. Calmly, almost solemnly, she said, "As teachers, you will teach as much with who you are as with what you know." That is why we are teachers. We treasure our art, cherish our students, reveal our hearts, embrace humanity, and touch the soul of eternity. Our passion for music is only equaled by our passion to help those who wish to learn its wonders.

ABOUT THE AUTHOR

Peter Loel Boonshaft holds Bachelor of Music (Summa Cum Laude), Master of Music Education in Conducting, and Doctor of Musical Arts degrees. Dr. Boonshaft was also awarded a Connecticut General Fellowship for study at the Kodály Musical Training Institute, from which he holds a Certificate. He is currently on the faculty of Hofstra University in Hempstead, New York, where he is Professor of Music and Director of Bands. He is Conductor of the Hofstra University Wind Ensemble and Symphonic Band, professor of conducting and music education, and Director of the graduate wind conducting program. Prior to this appointment, Boonshaft was on the faculty of Moravian College and the University of Hartford. He was Founder and Music Director of the Pennsylvania Youth Honors Concert Band and the Connecticut Valley Youth Wind Ensemble. In addition, he held the post of Music Director and Conductor of the Metropolitan Wind Symphony of Boston.

Peter Boonshaft has been a consultant or recorded for Boosey & Hawkes Music Publishers, Southern Music Publishers, Kendor Music Publishers, Daehn Publications, and C. Allen Music. Active as a proponent of new literature for concert band, he has commissioned and conducted over thirty world premieres by such notable composers as W. Francis McBeth, Johan de Meij, Fisher Tull, H. Owen Reed, Vaclav Nelhybel, David Gillingham, Philip Sparke, Andrew Boysen, Robert W. Smith, David Holsinger, Robert Washburn, Elliot Del Borgo, Herbert Deutsch, Robert Hawkins, Larry Lipkis, Ian McDougall, Reber Clark, Gregory Sanders, Roland Barrett and Jared Spears. Boonshaft is also the author of *Vaclav Nelhybel: His Life and Works,* the only authorized biography of the composer, and articles for *Instrumentalist Magazine,* the *National Band Association Journal,* MENC's *Teaching Music* and *Band Director's Guide.* In addition, he holds the post of Band/Wind Ensemble Editor for the *School Music News.* Among the soloists who have appeared in performance with him are John Marcellus, Harvey Phillips, Ed Shaughnessy, Lynn Klock, Don Butterfield, Dave Steinmeyer and the United States Air Force "Airmen of Note," Chester Schmitz, and the Vienna Schubert Trio.

Boonshaft has been awarded membership in Pi Kappa Lambda and Alpha Chi, as well as twice receiving the University of Hartford Regent's Award and that University's Outstanding Music Educator Award. He has received official proclamations from the Governors of four states and a Certificate of Appreciation from President Ronald Reagan, as well as performing for President and Mrs. George Bush, and for Margaret Thatcher, Former Prime Minister of the United Kingdom. His honors also include being selected three times as a National Endowment for the Arts "Artist in Residence", three times awarded Honorary Life Membership in the Tri-M Music Honor Society, and being selected for the Center for Scholarly Research and Academic Excellence at Hofstra University. Extremely active as a guest conductor and clinician for festivals, concerts, and workshops nationally and internationally, he was chosen to conduct the All-Eastern Band for the MENC Eastern Division Conference in Baltimore, Maryland; as a clinician for the National Convention of the Canadian Music Educators Association in Halifax, Nova Scotia; as conductor of the All-Eastern Directors Band for the MENC Eastern Division Conference in New York City; as guest conductor and clinician for the European Music Educators Convention in Heidelberg, Germany; as a clinician and speaker for the National Convention of the American School Band Directors Association in Honolulu, Hawaii; as a clinician for the MENC Northwest Division Conference in Spokane, Washington; was named conductor of the MENC National High School Honors Band for the National Convention in Nashville, Tennessee; as guest conductor of the Goldman Memorial Band; as conductor of the All-Northwest Band for the MENC Northwest Division Conference in Portland, Oregon; and recently received invitations to conduct in China and Brazil.